Drunken History

Drunken History

Clint Lanier & Derek Hembree

AO Media LLC

Copyright © 2012 Clint Lanier and Derek Hembree

All rights reserved.

No part of this book may be used or reproduced in any manner whatsoever without the written permission of the Publisher.

Printed in the United States of America. For information address

AO Media LLC, 2263 S. Main St. Las Cruces, NM 88005

Library of Congress Cataloging-in-Publication Data

Lanier, Clint and Hembree, Derek

Drunken History

ISBN 978-0615672731

1. Humor. 2. History. 3. Culture.

AO Media LLC books are available for bulk purchase and promotion. For details contact info@aomedia-llc.com.

Design is Copyright © 2012 AO Media LLC

Design by Martin Riggenbach-http://www.zensatori.net

All images public domain through Wikimedia.org unless otherwise indicated.

First Paperback Edition

To Regina, to Mandy, and to each other!

Contents

Foreword

Plato is quoted as once saying "He was a wise man who invented beer," and we couldn't agree more.

For more than a year, we have been researching and sharing mankind's history with the fermentation and distillation of alcohol. Few things in this world have we (meaning mankind) celebrated or owed so much to while at the same time tried to hide like some dirty little secret.

So what do we owe to alcohol? Well, discovering America would have never taken place without beer. When Christopher Columbus sailed west looking for a shortcut to Asia, water could not be stored for long periods, but beer could. Sailors and explorers like Columbus and Magellan took beer and spirits instead of pure water as their main and sometimes only source of drinkable liquid. This same practice was used on the Mayflower.

Trying to brew a better beer or distill a finer spirit also led to innovations we take for granted today. Take pasteurization for example. Loius Pasteur, the father of pasteurization, wasn't looking for a way to make milk safer to drink. He was looking for a way to increase the shelf life of beer when he discovered pasteurization and its many uses.

In the realm of money, governments, the United States alone brings in over 6 billion dollars in yearly tax revenue on fermented drink, and that's just one aspect. Can you imagine how many jobs owe their existence to distillation, fermentation, and the consumption of these drinks? From factory workers, brewers, distillers, truck drivers, business owners, even the guy standing behind the bar serving you a cold one, they're all jobs created by and for alcohol.

And one can never really breach the subject of alcohol without mentioning prohibition. Though there are few places it is more "celebrated" than in the U.S., prohibition was also tested in Russia, Iceland, Norway, and Australia to name just a few.

Historically governments have probably never enacted a less popular or more destructive law. In combination, prohibition-type laws have only led to organized crime and made criminals out of the everyday hard working men and women of their respective countries. In short, they were imposed by the few onto the many and were failures paid for by the common man.

In our search, we found that alcohol, in one form or another has been an ever-present aspect of mankind's existence for more than 10,000 years. And yet today it seems to have been swept under the rug, hidden, and even at times ignored and vilified when we look back on mankind's history.

Drunken History reopens this once closed chapter of our existence and shows it's nothing to be ashamed of. It should be celebrated, enjoyed, and consumed much like the beverages created over 10,000 years ago.

So join us in this easy and fun-to-read book as we take you on a journey from the earliest discovery of fermentation right up until today. From ancient Samaria, the Roman Empire,

America's Founding Fathers, and the world's breweries and distilleries, we visit every available aspect of man and his historical infatuation with alcohol. Cheer!

A note about our research. The collection in this book was gathered over the course of a year from a slew of sources. There is a new fact or figure presented in just about every other sentence, and if we'd included source notes, the book would read like the Bible and the references section would be half as long as the book itself.

We welcome you to verify the facts we present, or ask us where we found them: we'd be happy to let you know.

The Beginning

(Pre-800 AD)

We don't know how we discovered alcohol. It happened some time ago though. Experts estimate that around 10,000 BC something miraculous occurred. Somebody drank something that made them wobble. The first taste by mankind of a fermented beverage.

Imagine! Having never had alcohol in your system and then drinking it for the first time. What was existence like before that first sip? Probably pretty dull. There was the daily avoidance of bears and tigers and lions and all sorts of things that wanted to eat you. There was the struggle to eke out survival by gathering nuts and twigs. There were communal hunts of wooly mammoths and then skinning of the beasts with stone knives and crude implements.

In other words, life was hard. What did they do for recreation? Play dominos or board games? Probably not. Night would most likely find them cowering in a cave, chipping pictures in the wall and being terrified by the sounds outside that were strange and evil.

Then at some point (according to historians) the following happened. A bowl or other vessel was filled with wild grains collected during gathering (remember they didn't yet grow crops). The bowl sat outside or was otherwise exposed to the elements. The bowl and its contents became dampened—not soaked because the grains had to get just wet enough to germinate and increase their sugar content.

Then the bowl became filled with water, making a porridge or stew. This is when wild yeast settled on it and the fermentation process began.

Think of the look on the face of the first person to sip from that bowl, wobble a bit and then look at it wondering what the hell this new and wonderful creation was. Was it from the gods? How was it made? More importantly, how do we make more?

With absolutely no resistance to alcohol even the slightest amount would have gotten them drunk. This of course leads one to imagine what the reactions of the others were.

"Hey, what the hell's wrong with Og? He act funny..."

This section takes a look at the earliest periods of our species and at some of the most significant regions of civilization around the world. Evidence of drinking, and drinking to get drunk, has been found throughout.

If nothing else this chapter demonstrates it's nothing new.

The historical estimate is that we started boozing 10,000 years ago. *Proof* of intentional fermentation however was found in Northern China dating as far back as 7000 BC (9000 years ago). Pottery vessels were found containing a mixture of mead, rice and other fruits along with organic compounds of fermentation.

Similarly, evidence of beer—crudely made beer—has been found on 7000 year old pottery shards uncovered in Sumerian towns in what is now Iran (which is somehow ironic).

Additionally, archaeologists have further found evidence that Neolithic houses (about 8,500 BC), again in Iran, had as much as 54 liters of wine on hand at a time. 54 liters! That's about 14 gallons to those of us in the U.S. Preparations for the impromptu party, or just the daily beverage?

This is about the beginning of wine-making as well. Historians think Neolithic man—specifically in this region—watched other animals get silly after drinking naturally fermented grapes, and then also tried them.

Much of this also came before other culinary innovation. Archeologists even suggest people were brewing beer 2000 years before they were baking bread. Beer and bread are made with the exact same ingredients, so teetotalers can't credit that to lack of resources. When push comes to shove, which would you rather have?

In fact, experts further believe that the purpose for producing grain crops was for the production of beer. Thus, beer led us from a hunting-gathering society to one of harvesters—settled and building civilizations and society.

We'll look at these ancient periods geographically, simply to show that boozing it up wasn't isolated to one area. It either spread or was discovered naturally throughout the world.

In either case making and drinking fermented beverages was as natural as breathing.

The Middle East

The Middle East has evidence of some of the oldest civilizations on earth. Mankind crawled from the caves and created villages, grew crops, dug wells and domesticated animals all in this region of the world about 10,000 years ago.

Innovation took place as well. After all, early mathematics, geometry and architecture still influence our world today.

In this part of the world, and in the earliest periods for which we have history, we also find innovations in alcohol. From what they drank to the way they drank it, the days of Og and Ig in the cave slurping clay bowls of grain porridge were over. Here we see the first vineyards, breweries, and recreational drinking.

Let's start our journey with what came first according to the Bible: the word. The oldest known written language— cuneiform from about 30th century BC and emerging in Sumer—has over 160 terms for beer.

Cuneiform tablet from Samaria showing beer allocation.

And similarly, the earliest recorded recipe discovered is a 3900 year old beer recipe found written on a Sumerian tablet. The recipe—a hymn actually—described how the 18th century BC Sumerian goddess, Ninkasi, made beer for us humans. Only natural because she was the goddess of beer, after all. According to their myths, Ninkasi, whose name meant "you fill my mouth" was formed by the greater gods to "satisfy desire and sate the heart."

Some of the earliest depictions of people drinking also date from this society. Sumerian tablets found by archeologists depict groups of people drinking from communal bowls using reed straws.

The First Recipe for Beer

You are the one who handles the dough with a big shovel,

Mixing in a pit, the bappir with sweet aromatics,

Ninkasi, you are the one who handles the dough with a big shovel,

Mixing in a pit, the bappir with honey,

You are the one who bakes the bappir in the big oven,

Puts in order the piles of hulled grains,

Ninkasi, you are the one who waters the malt set on the ground,

The noble dogs keep away even the potentates,

You are the one who soaks the malt in a jar,

The waves rise, the waves fall.

You are the one who spreads the cooked mash on large reed mats,

Coolness overcomes,

You are the one who holds with both hands the great sweet wort,

The filtering vat, which makes a pleasant sound,

You place appropriately on a large collector vat.

Ninkasi, you are the one who pours out the filtered beer of the collector vat,

Like the onrush of Tigris and Euphrates.

The beer they were drinking was unfiltered, and so historians think that the straws were used to help filter the grit from the good stuff. Archeologists also believe this was the first use of the straw, invented to drink beer.

Some of the oldest examples of written texts ever discovered—also Sumerian from a later period, 4000-3000 BC—contain recipes for brewing beer. Sumerians had a variety of beer types while the Babylonians (not to distant from Sumer) had at least 20 different kinds.

And close to the same period, in the Epic of Gilgamesh, an epic poem from 2000 BC Mesopotamia—the region containing Sumer and Babylon—and amongst the earliest surviving works of literature, the savage king, Enkidu, is civilized by a woman who teaches him to eat bread and drink beer. Civilization, or at least being civil, was to drink beer.

Throughout the region, between 3000 and 2000 BC in Mesopotamia, 40% of all grains were used for brewing beer instead of making bread or other food. Some historians have called it a surplus commodity, made when there were more ingredients than needed. But, a consistent surplus of 40% simply sounds like good planning.

What's really interesting is that throughout history, mead—fermented honey—has been made by every society/race/tribe living close enough to local vegetation supporting bees, and that especially applies to the societies of the Middle East. Think about it. Nearly every civilization, without contacting each other, somehow discovered that honey ferments. What's more, they pursued fermenting honey for their own regular consumption.

They seemed to treasure mead at this period, and it was often used in cultural rituals. For example, in ancient Babylon the bride's father supplied the groom with mead, honey beer, for one lunar month after the marriage (and so the term honeymoon was created).

In 2100 BC, the Babylonian king Hammurabi began creating laws specifically about brewing and selling beer. Included in his Code of Hammurabi, one of the oldest examples of written laws, were regulations for tavern keepers. These detailed how much to charge for beer and set standards for their quality. There were also stiff penalties for barkeeps who tried to gouge their customers.

In most early societies, alcohol production was overseen by religious leaders or groups. Actually this is true all the way up until the 15th century, AD. But it was especially true in Babylon. King Hammurabi declared a daily beer ration for all in his kingdom, and thought especially high of his priests. They were allotted a ration of five liters per day (about 1.3 gallons), compared with workers and lay people, who were given two liters a day (about a half a gallon).

Love for beer continued for a long time in Babylon. In 200 AD Jewish captives in Babylon recorded drinking *sicera ex luplis confectam*, or strong drink made from hops. We imagine this to be beer, and if it is, it's pretty significant considering the use of hops in beer didn't become popular in Europe until the 16th century.

In this region, and in this period, we see the antics of people no different than the antics of drunks today. Even in the Bible. According to Genesis, the first three things Noah did after finding dry land were to plant a vineyard, make wine, and then get drunk. In fact he got so drunk that he passed out naked, something that is still regularly occurring in frat houses throughout the country.

Egypt

Ancient Egyptians loved beer. It was the national drink, enjoyed by the poor and the rich alike. It was given to servants, slaves, workers, wives and children. It was enjoyed at weddings, funerals, for breakfast, lunch and dinner. Not only that, but it was seen as noble, befitting royalty and given to them by the gods.

Um..more wine? Hieroglyph from Egypt.

Here, in ancient Egypt, we see the quasi-commercialization of beer. They built dedicated breweries, grew crops specifically for beer, and looked at it as a commodity. People were designated to make it (early brewers), and we see written records about how much people drank, where and when.

The birth of mankind's love for beer, in other words, was in Egypt about 7000 years ago.

This was how important beer was to them. Egyptian pharaohs had to guarantee their wives an allotment of two crocks (one gallon) of beer per day before they would wed. This was perhaps symbolically saying that the pharaoh would always provide for the bride, especially the necessities of life. Beer was, after all, a necessity.

It was a necessity for daily life, but also for the afterlife, especially for the common folk. While ancient Egyptian Pharaohs were entombed with gold and jewels, workers were buried with bread and beer for the afterlife (though when King Scorpion I of Egypt died about 3000 BC he was buried with *700* jars of wine to help him cross the river).

There was also an Egyptian tradition dating to 1600 BC that demanded a man marry a woman if he offered her a sip of his beer. Drinking beer in Egypt was taken seriously (so seriously in fact that many wealthy served beer in gold cups).

And, in order to secure the woman's hand for marriage, the suitor would present the bride-to-be's father with the always appreciated gift of beer. This was perhaps in the same tradition as the Pharaoh guaranteeing a supply of beer as a necessity.

The love for beer also made ancient Egypt a great place to get sick. A medical text dating from 1600 BC includes 100 remedies that feature the use of beer as medicine or as an ingredient for healing.

Likewise it was also used for payment for both goods and services. History doesn't know if those who built the ancient pyramids were slaves or not, but we do know they were paid in beer. Records actually show that the workers who built the Egyptian pyramids were paid one gallon of beer every day during the building either as incentive or reward. In fact they were given these as rations three times per day while working.

This could be the cause of certain etchings on stones that have been identified and translated by historians. One worker's inscription on the Great Pyramid of Giza, built for King Khufu (2560 BC), reads "The crew of Khufu is drunk." The worker or workers actually got drunk and then inscribed this graffiti into the stone (or at the very least thought it humorous to tell others about their condition).

Although beer and wine were both viewed as simple necessities of life, intoxication itself might not have been thought of so highly. The first written record of someone being intoxicated was preserved in hieroglyphics dating back to 1300 BC. Apparently Pharaoh Seti I charged a worker with being too drunk to work. We can't help but wonder if it was Khufu's crew (dates are wrong, but the evidence was certainly incriminating).

One might wonder why so much attention was paid to the crude drink they must have been drinking back then. But, according to what historians and archeologists have found, ancient Egyptians actually knew their alcohol. Evidence suggests they made at least 17 varieties of beer and at least 24 varieties of wine. While these might not seem like much, think of the word, "variety" versus "brand." Almost 90% of the best selling beers in the United States are the same variety: lagers. Comparatively, the Egyptians might have had a better variety than we do today.

And Egyptian beer was popular to more than just the Egyptians. In the 18th century BC Egyptian Pharaoh Amenemhet III stopped a mass migration of starving Nubians traveling into Egypt by sending them bread and beer. This was apparently enough to make them happy because history shows they turned back and the King wasn't faced with a horde of starving people invading his land.

In Egypt at this time, beer was more than just a drink. It was a way of life and part of the fabric of their culture, even touching their religious beliefs. In Egyptian mythology the goddess Hathor went on a rampage to avenge her father, Ra. She became mad with blood-lust and was murdering all of the people she could find. Ra realized he needed to stop her, and the only method he could find was to dye beer red like blood and create a lake with it. Hathor drank the lake dry, became drunk, and stopped her rampage.

Wine and beer were both important to the life of the Egyptian in the ancient world. In fact in the later years of the kingdom, wine was the preferred drink, especially for the wealthy, but beer still remained important.

As a closing statement to the importance of wine and beer, consider this. Most gods were worshiped regionally, so in one part of the kingdom people might offer sacrifices to one but not the other. Then there was Osiris who was worshiped by everyone. Osiris was the god of wine and taught the people how to brew beer.

To finish off Egypt in the ancient world, it is important to mention that it is in Egypt that we see the earliest potential evidence of distillation. Jars dating from 1850 BC were found with traces of distilled spirits. But the contents of the jars were probably not consumed. Experts think the first distillation was for making perfume, not for making drink. In either case, mankind was advancing.

China and Asia

Asia is where the oldest evidence of alcohol is found, and the history here is rich in its variety and love for fermented beverages of all kind. Interestingly, unlike other areas, Asia is found to have many different types of beverages all as popular as the next.

Though some of the oldest evidence of human's consumption of fermented beverages comes from China, they seemed torn about how much they appreciated it. For example, in China between 1400 and 1100 BC, laws against making wine were made and then repealed 41 times. During that time, in 1116 BC, a Chinese Imperial edict even stated that alcohol was prescribed by heaven for man's enjoyment in moderation.

Maybe it was this last part of the edict that caused the problems: moderation. As in Egypt and elsewhere, drinking was simply part of the culture. It was tradition to drink wine at funerals, at political events, at religious ceremonies, and before battle. In short, for just about every occasion. There would have to be a fine line between sobriety and drunkenness.

Especially since there was a lot of evidence of competitive drinking (meaning drinking games) in China, specifically during the Tang Dynasty—about 600-900 BC. Players drew lots from a canister and had to go through a series of trials depending on the lot. It could be something as simple as taking the number of drinks indicated on the lot, or something more complicated, like answering a riddle.

There were also rules according to who the player was, like considerations for the youngest player, the oldest player, the richest, etc. It doesn't seem like drinking games are conducive to a society trying to stay sober. But in any case, competitive drinking was also, apparently, part of their culture.

Maybe the one drink most well known to Asia is Sake. Sake is actually a beer because it's made with rice, a grain, and not a fruit. It was first mentioned in a text called Kojiki, Japan's first written history, which was recorded in 712 AD.

However evidence of rice in traces of the oldest fermented beverages found in history (located in China) indicate they used rice as a source for booze long, long before this. Our next two stops are two of the oldest and most respected civilizations in history.

Greece and Rome

Ancient Greeks are typically viewed as some of the most enlightened people in history. Much of our own philosophies and beliefs, theories about science and nature, and even mathematical calculations, stem from the knowledge they left behind.

When it comes to how the Ancient Greeks viewed beer we don't have a lot to go on. We know because of the similarity of their words for beer that it was probably brought from Egypt, a much earlier society that the Greeks visited. The word for beer in Egyptian is zytum and in Greek it is zythos.

There are some sources that suggest very early on in Greek civilization they drank beer, but soon after switched to wine once it was discovered and perfected. The first evidence of Greek winemaking dates from 1600 BC, so they had begun very early in their history. The

Silenus, Greek god of Drunkenness.

sophistication of the wine-press found from this date indicates they probably got the technology elsewhere for making wine as well.

So wine they did drink, and there is much evidence to suggest this—from wine vessels to an extensive history about wine growing and making in different regions.

We also know they believed more in temperance than in getting drunk. They often mixed their wine with water to dilute it and held a belief that drunkenness was not enlightened.

However, it is around 900-700 BC we begin to see references to Dionysos, the god of wine, mostly from poems and epics by Homer. Within a few hundred years historians start finding evidence of cult-like worship for Dionysos. In other words, cults were set up to worship the god of wine, and celebrate not only the drink but also the act of drinking and the state of drunkenness. Followers believed drinking brought them closer to their deity.

Then there was Silenus the Greek god of drunkenness and drinking companions. He was actually the drinking companion of Dionysos and most often tanked out of his mind. In fact, he usually had to be carried by people or a donkey to get around because he couldn't even walk. But when drunk, he became wise and prophetic. Interestingly this is how most people think they are when drunk even today.

Greek philosophers also often mentioned drink and drinking. Sophocles (496-406 BC) for example recommended a diet of bread, meat, vegetables and beer to stay healthy. And the Greek Historian Xenophon in 400 BC described Persian beer as strong when not mixed with water and very good if the person drinking it is used to it. This actually ties into a point made at the beginning that most Greeks would often dilute their drink with water. Persians, apparently, didn't share that technique.

We also get the earliest recorded hangover cure from a Greek from this period. In 479 BC the Greek philosopher, Antiphanes, suggested that to cure a hangover the best thing people could do is drink more wine the next day. Antiphanes was ahead of his time, obviously.

Such hangover cures might have come in handy to some, more recreational drinkers in Greece. Written records suggest people were playing drinking games at least 2500 year ago. Of all people, Plato in his Symposium includes a section called, *The Drinking Party*, where he details a simple game of drinking a bowl full of wine and then passing it on.

Thankfully there were more sophisticated games as well. One particularly popular one was called, Kottabos. Players, all men, while lounging on chaise-like chairs, either spit or threw wine (or the dregs of a wine glass) at targets in the room, getting points for things like hitting the target, knocking the target to the ground, or not having a break in their spit or throw.

While popular opinion is that the Greeks were very temperate, recording that they should dilute beverages with water, one must believe that for the most part, people drank and got drunk just like they do now (if not more and more frequently).

The choice of beverages—and in fact the whole approach to alcohol—was much the same for the Romans as well: wine, not beer. However, they did not have the same early qualms with drinking as the Greeks portended to.

On the contrary, drinking to get drunk was celebrated, enjoyed by gods, and looked on as a common occurrence.

For example, in the 2nd century AD, Rome was the largest importer of wine in the world, and annual per capita consumption peaked at 250 liters per person per year. Contrast this with 2010's statistics for the highest three wine consuming countries, ranging from 52.5 to 54.8 liters per capita. That's almost five times as much wine consumed per person!

Beer, on the other hand was simply not enjoyed by the Romans at all, but that didn't mean they didn't come into contact with it. Julius Caesar notes that the Suevi Germanic tribe drank beer—a lot of beer—as their main beverage. He also stated they didn't drink wine because they believed it rendered the drinker effeminate.

The 4th century AD Roman Emperor Julian thought little of not only beer, but also the people who drank it as well. He wrote that wine was like nectar given to them from the gods, while beer on the other hand makes the drinker smell like a "Billy-goat."

But, oddly enough, it is the Romans who are credited with advancing beer to other parts of Europe. In approximately 55 BC Romans introduced the drink to northern Europe, especially Britain and northern France (it was already being consumed by the Germanic people, but those in northern Europe were primarily drinking mead).

The favor was returned when in the 5th century AD Rome was still carrying wine in clay jars. The Celts taught the Romans how to make the wooden barrels they were using to store beer. They were easier to carry of course (not as fragile), but the flaw was that they allowed wine to spoil, unlike the clay jars which could keep wine for years without affecting its composition. Romans had to drink their wine more quickly, which as it turned out, was not such a bad thing.

60 BC Recipe for Mead

Take rainwater kept for several years, and mix a sextarius of this water with a pound of honey. For a weaker mead, mix a sextarius of water with nine ounces of honey. The whole is exposed to the sun for 40 days, and then left on a shelf near the fire. If you have no rain water, then boil spring water.

Though Romans shied away from beer, they did drink mead, the fermented honey beverage consumed by just about every other civilization and people on earth at one time. One of the earliest recipes recorded for mead was actually written by the Roman philosopher and historian, Columella in his 12 volumes, *De Re Rustica,* written about 60 BC.

Europe

As civilizations spread throughout the earth, so did their secrets to fermentation, brewing and wine-making.

In Europe we see evidence of transplanted preferences for alcohol. We see wine brought from Rome and beer from the Middle East. We see methods for making alcoholic beverages imported as well.

We also see native discoveries as well as early societies drinking easily made beverages like mead, or honey-wine. We lastly see the foundation that later innovations, like beer-making and distilling, would be based on.

The oldest existing style of beer in the world was additionally made during this time: the Lambic, which originated in Belgium around 3000-2500 BC, and ferments by wild yeasts. Historians think Lambic style beer was created by accident. They theorize that a kind of porridge was left out and then naturally fermented by the yeast native to that one particular region in Europe. True Lambics, then, only come from this single part of the world because of that natural, wild yeast.

But drinking any kind of alcoholic beverage appears to be popular at this time. Throughout central Europe in fact, dating from 3500 BC, archeologists found a huge number of drinking cups, indicating to them that there was a rise in the number of beer or mead-drinking cults at that time. Whole religious movements were dedicated to fermented beverages.

Beer-making and fermenting was prevalent everywhere, it seems. During this time in Scotland the base of very early Scotch whisky was being made. Scottish ale that was first made by the Picts (native Scots) around 2000 BC was a simple ale made from malt and yeast and flavored with local herbs, and also later distilled and turned into Scotch.

And at an archaeological dig in Turkey, archeologists found traces of an ancient beer, wine and mead beverage in a 700 BC tomb. As it turned out, it was the tomb of the real King Midas, ruler of Phyrgia in the 8th century BC. He was buried with 157 drinking vessels and jugs of beer. The residue of this drink was analyzed and the recipe was copied by the craft beer company, Dog Fish Head for their specialty beer, *Midas Touch*.

Similarly in Bavaria archaeologists found the tomb of a local tribal leader from 800 BC who had been buried with crocks of beer as well as ingredients for brewing. This is actually quite smart: when he runs out of beer in the afterlife he can just make another batch with the ingredients he was left with.

Another interesting find was a 2000-year old wooden tankard uncovered in Wales in 2007. What makes this find so special was that it was wooden and survived so long, and it also had a 4 pint capacity. That's a half a gallon of drink—most likely ale or mead—at a time.

The afterlife was much on people's minds at this time, as superstition and mythology ruled a lot of Europe. Included in that mythology was typically a figure or being that quenched mankind's thirst in one way or another. In ancient Czech mythology, Radegast was the god of both hospitality and mutuality. Naturally he was responsible for creating beer.

In ancient Lithuania, not only did they have a god for beer (Raugutis), but they also had one just for fermentation, Raugupatis. In ancient Finnish mythology Kalevatar mixed bear saliva and wild honey to create the gift of ale. In most all cases, fermented beverages were a *gift* from the gods, not a punishment or something commonplace.

And ancient Europeans appreciated it. For over 1000 years Scandinavian tribes brewed a special Yule beer just for the winter solstice celebrations. The beer was stronger than other batches, and included special ingredients.

Similarly, during their summer solstice celebrations, Vikings would hallow (original word halwen) or honor the gods with ale or mead. Not by sacrifice, but by drinking. In other words, the simple act of drinking was the act of worshiping their gods.

In short, then, Europe in the earliest age of man was active and inventive when it came to alcohol and drinking. Drinking was a celebration, a form of honoring the living, the dead and the deities. It was an important part of life, only to become even more important in centuries to come.

South America

Though brief in the amount of records we have, it is important to include what little there is about alcohol in early South America, if merely to demonstrate that booze was enjoyed by all people around the globe (just as it is today).

One of the earliest and perhaps most surprising finds was evidence of a crude wine made from cacao pods that dates back to at least 1400 BC. You work with what you have, and the indigenous people of South America certainly had cacao in abundance, so it was only natural. It's almost ironic that wineries have recently begun making chocolate-infused wine in the past two decades. South Americans had them beat by three millennia.

Most common in South America, though, was pulque. Pulque—a type of beer made with fermented corn—was known throughout South America and drank frequently at all religious ceremonies and festivals.

Patecatl, god of fermentation.

As in other cultures, the Aztec believed that pulque was a divine gift. In fact it was

Tezcatzontecatl, the Aztec god of pulque, who bestowed this wonderful drink. Additionally he was helped by the god of fermentation, Patecatl. Together they provided the drink used at religious and other types of ceremonies, and even made and consumed today.

Of course Tezcatzontecatl was also the god of drunkenness and (ironically enough) fertility. The Aztecs, it would seem, were well ahead of the age they were living in.

To end this period of our history, we should look at perhaps the keystone fact that highlights the prevalence of alcohol—beer, wine and even spirits—in the lives of men and women of that time. Scholars suggest that fermented beverages were so common to the Incas that making someone drink water was considered a form of punishment.

If that isn't enough to illustrate what life was like at this point, nothing is.

The Middle Ages

800 AD—1300 AD

The Middle Ages were the defining time in the history of beer-making (and to a lesser extent, in distillation). Up to this point, much of man's quest to quench his thirst was dictated by nature—wild yeasts, seasonal crops and ingredients.

Also up to this point we see little consistency or quality control. Most all alcohol production was local and small, though in some large societies (like Rome, for example), we see large commercial wine-making ventures. And, in other places—like royal courts around the world—we see larger wine-making operations as well.

For the most part, however, people brewed or fermented for personal consumption and in their own houses.

As such, the stuff was most likely awful. The alcoholic porridge that Og and Ig drank in the cave was probably much better (in terms of ingredients) than what people in European towns and villages of the Middle Ages used. After all, sewage, waste and all sorts of filth were typically dumped into their water systems.

This is one reason for the high consumption of ale at this time throughout Europe. Water was simply unhealthy. But ale was not—the water was boiled after all.

However, it spoiled easily and did not keep very long. This changed in the 400 years that mark what we call the Middle Ages.

Another change was the move to true distillation which occurred during this period. Mankind discovered *aqua vitae*, or water of life (known today as whiskey).

In fact the first record of drinking whiskey is when Henry II of England visited Ireland in 1174 and drank what was written officially in the record as *aquae vitae*.

And we—mankind that is—liked it. Hell we loved it! Whole economies were created with this discovery.

The Middle Ages were the catalyst for much of what we have, and even more of what we drink.

The Middle Ages in General

In the Middle Ages, beer—and generally speaking any alcohol—was used for just about everything, touching everybody's lives in a number of important and even curious ways. Witches for example mixed Alexandrian gum, liquid alum, and garden crocus with two cups of beer as a contraceptive. We're not sure if this worked, though, as the evidence seems awfully thin, but we're guessing probably not. This is a fairly extreme example, but serves the point.

In general, though, in medieval England beer-making was a woman's job and if the beer spoiled or sickened people the women who made it were accused of witchery. This is where we get terms such as, "witches *brew*" and "*brew*-witch." As brewesses, women had considerable authority, especially considering the amount of beer people drank.

In fact, English statutes for brewing fraud—selling spoiled or bad beer, or overcharging for beer—outlines punishments for women brewers but not men (most likely because men rarely brewed). During this time the brewess wasn't even able to determine her own price for ale. The price of beer (in England anyway) was determined by official *gustatores cervisiae* (court ale-tasters). They would first taste the beer to check its quality and then determine how much the brewess could charge.

Men didn't really brew commercially at this time, while women, in contrast would often sell surplus beer that the household would not drink. This would serve as extra income for the household but would be a source of contention in coming years.

In 1286 the Duke of Holland decreed that wives had the right to brew whatever volume of beer they desired. This was most likely a response to a rise in commercial brewing (by men most often) and the corresponding complaints about competition from women brewers at home. The Duke, apparently, took pity on the tradition of the brew-wife and showed the commercial brewers how little influence they had. That would change in the next couple of hundred years.

The further industrialization of brewing in the 11th—14th centuries made men responsible for making beer, and so the age of the woman-brewer went into obscurity.

Brewing itself, though, and the product of brewing was to go through a ton of changes before the end of the Middle Ages. Everything from the way beer was brewed to the tools used and even the ingredients would undergo substantial shifts.

Before brewers used hops in their beer (which didn't happen regularly until the 16th century), they used gruit, a combination of herbs like horehound, ivy and mugwort. The combination of ingredients, plus grains and water created the basis for what they called ale. Ale in fact, strictly speaking, is un-hopped beer.

But according to some historians, the problem with ale was that without the preserving qualities of hops it was prone to spoiling often. This (combined with a complete lack of understanding about sanitation) was most often the reason ale would spoil so quickly and sicken people.

There is evidence though that hopped beer had been around for awhile, such as the reference to it by Jewish Babylonian prisoners in the early millennium. However the first explicit mention of the use of hops in brewing in Europe is from Germany in 1079, so it did take a while to catch on.

As in previous societies, though, drinking and getting drunk was apparently a common occurrence. Medieval folklore even had 4 successive stages of drunkenness based on the animals it made men resemble. These were (in order) sheep, lion, ape, and then finally, the sow.

The stamina of drinkers in those days must have been fantastic, especially considering the episodes and statistics recorded in history.

Gambrinus could drink a keg at a time.

For example, during a seven day celebration in Russia in 996 AD, attendants went through 300 large wooden tubs or about 5000 liters of mead. And in Florence during roughly the same time, wine consumption was about 10 barrels per capita per year.

Another example is found in the legend of the Bavarian Beer King named Gambrinus from the 12th century. It tells of a Duke who drank an entire keg of beer to demonstrate his stamina. He was then made a king for his feat. That is what people of the day respected.

Pubs—or Public Houses—were also beginning to become commonplace. These were in essence the first bars (though quite different than those we see today), and were frequented by the thirsty just as they are today. The Brazen Head Pub in Dublin is still standing, and is over 800 years old (first opened in the 13th century), making the oldest in the U.S. (White Horse Tavern founded in 1673) look like a toddler.

But the oldest drinking establishment in the world is Sean's Bar in Athlone Ireland. There has been a pub on that spot since 900 AD.

Perhaps some thought pubs were becoming too numerous though. In 965 King Edgar declared there should be no more than one per village. This law would be replaced not too long after it was established, but points to a trend we see throughout history to limit the supply of booze for the common man.

By the 13th century, however, it was common for courts of law to be conducted in taverns throughout Europe. Edgar's decree was eventually forgotten altogether. Well, for a while anyway.

Beer during this time also became an international commercial product. Brewers in Bremen, Hamburg and Wismar Germany began exporting beer for sale as early as 1200 AD. This is an indicator of its growing importance to all walks of life and society. Beer was becoming less of something simply to drink as a replacement for water, and more a choice for connoisseurs.

To quench the thirst of these connoisseurs, Bremen Germany had over 600 breweries in 1500 AD (with a population of only 25,000). They were regularly exporting beer to Holland, England and even India.

Specialty beers were also becoming popular during the Middle Ages. Though Scandinavians had already prepared special ales for winter or summer solstice celebrations, these seasonal beers were just starting to find a following in Europe as well.

The French tradition of Biere Noel, for example, comes from the 11th century. Brewers made a special, spiced beer to celebrate the holidays. It was made and sold on only this special occasion, but it points to a desire for variety and taste.

And also in the 11th century in Norway, grain farmers were required by law to brew a special beer for Christmas or be *ostracized* by the church. Beer was that important to them.

Its importance wasn't just limited to Europe. In South America researchers uncovered a 1000 year old brewery with a capacity to make 475 gallons of corn beer per week. Beer (or other regional, fermented beverages) was a staple throughout the world at this time.

Beer also became commoditized, used as a substitute for money on many occasions. There are records showing that in the 11th century in England, ale and beer were often accepted for rent by the ruling class and for taxes by royalty.

In fact a Welsh law from the 10th century taxed farmers one vat of mead, two vats of spiced ale, or four vats of "common ale" during harvest season, giving insight into which was valued more.

Beer as tax revenue wasn't isolated to England, though. In 1100 AD in China, the taxes on alcohol were one of the treasury's largest sources of income (flash forward to another section, the same was true for the United States until income taxes became law).

Alcohol and the Early Church

Much of the history of alcohol and alcoholic beverages in the Middle Ages concerns the Catholic Church. Not because nobody else around the world was fermenting or drinking, but because the innovations primarily came from the Church.

Think about that for a moment. Almost all of the important innovations in brewing, fermenting and distilling that occurred for a period of about 500 years happened in the Catholic Church. How is that possible?

For the most part it's because of the Benedictine monasteries that began appearing throughout Europe beginning in about 500 AD. The Benedictines believed in self-sufficiency and as much as possible tried to make everything they needed themselves. This included beer, wine and spirits.

So, for at least 500 years groups of monks with nothing else to do all day but think about how to make booze better, did just that.

But more than this, fermented beverages, specifically beer, entered a commercial phase. Beer began to be used popularly for barter, to pay rents or tax-bills. Beer was also sold by a number of different organizations and entities, and when the period ended the perception of beer—and in fact all fermented beverages—changed. Suddenly what was before merely a household need or convenience was now a commodity.

Most all of these transformations are due to the Church, its views on brewing and its contributions to a drinking culture.

And brewing as an *art form* was most likely perfected by monks during the Middle Ages (so the story about Friar Tuck actually wasn't that far-fetched).

Breweries as production facilities to make beer were created by monasteries and other Christian institutions in the 7th-9th centuries, and flourished up until the 1300s and even the 1400s in some countries. Some of these monastic breweries are still around today.

These monasteries and churches originally began making beer for both the monks' consumption and as a form of payment to the Church, feudal lords, and laypeople for products and services needed. Remember, Benedict wanted them to be self-sufficient, and beer was a needed commodity since water was so filthy and quite unhealthy.

The earliest known depiction of one of these breweries is from the plan for the Abbey of St. Gall in Switzerland from the 8th century AD. It included very prominently a place dedicated to making beer.

Later, in 820 AD, the Bishop of Basle planned the "ideal monastery." It actually had three separate breweries that would make different types of beer for monks, travelers and peasants. It isn't clear whether this monastery was ever built or not, but it's telling to know that the ideal one had such a large brewing operation.

However, the 9th century Abbey of St. Gallen (in Germany) did have three breweries, not to mention a malt house, a milling room, and a kiln. In short, it had everything needed to make a lot of beer. It was, by the way, completely self-sufficient in its brewing operations.

The oldest breweries in the world actually stem from this period, and are typical of the type of monastic breweries built at that time. It's hard to say which is older because of their contended histories, but it would be either the Weihenstephan (built in 1040 AD), or the Weltenburg Abbey (built in 1050 AD) both located in Bavaria.

Even though they were charged with being self-sufficient, the monasteries often had to get permission from the Vatican or local lords to brew. The 1096 charter of the Abbey de Saint-Martin in Belgium, for example, included permission to brew beer to promote public health. Water at the time and in the area was dirty and could cause diseases, so the beer made by the monks was much healthier.

Similarly in 1040 the Weihenstephan Abbey in Germany was given the right to brew beer from local lords and the church. However, 20th century archeologists discovered a hop garden from 768 on the property, suggesting they were brewing under the radar when nobody was looking.

These monastic breweries were widespread throughout Europe, and would have dotted the countryside. Historians have found evidence of 12 *different* Middle Age monasteries in Yorkshire, England alone. Of the 12, 11 of them had breweries. That's a lot of public health!

And at their peak in Germany, between 800-1300 AD there were about 500 monasteries brewing beer.

In fact, European monasteries were the main source of beer until they drastically cut production in the 13th century. The ruling classes finally understood the monetary benefits of controlling beer production, and so they taxed or legislated monastic breweries out of existence. Beer production at this point was taken over by the merchant class, and beer finally became a truly commercial enterprise.

The lives of the monks themselves were also much affected by brewing and beer. During the Middle Ages many European monasteries allowed monks to drink up to 5 liters of beer a day. That's almost 1 ½ gallons of beer every single day as a standard ration!

Monks partied with 5 liters of beer per day!

What's more these rations were typically doubled over the Lenten period because monks took at vow of starvation for 40 days, and so the beer acted as liquid bread. Ironically most of these monasteries forbade wine during fasting but allowed the beer because they felt it was necessary for health.

The term "liquid bread" as a synonym for beer was actually coined in these Middle Age monasteries. After all, every single one of the ingredients they used to make bread, they also used to make their beer. And since they weren't allowed the bread while fasting, beer was a handy replacement.

But while the five-liter ration for monks sounds impressive, some medieval nunneries allowed nuns up to seven liters of beer a day.

So how much did these monasteries actually brew? Well, according to the Domesday Book of 1086 England—a record of a great survey taken that year—the monks of St Paul's Cathedral in London brewed 67,814 gallons of ale using barley, wheat and oats in that year.

An extensive set of records for the year 1283 at St. Paul's also exists, and shows that monks used 26 tons (52,000 pounds) of malted wheat, barley and oats all for brewing. In that year, again, brothers brewed almost 68,000 gallons of ale (they brewed 100 times during a typical year, with each batch yielding at least 678 gallons of beer).

They sold a total of only 37 gallons to people in the surrounding city. That means they consumed for themselves (or gave away to pilgrims, visitors and peasants) around 67,060 gallons throughout the year.

Records also show that St. Paul's regularly used the same amount of grain for brewing as it did for bread every year. So liquid bread, apparently was just as important as real bread (though, maybe enjoyed more).

What's really fun is that experts also believe that the beer they brewed would have been about 12% alcohol by volume. The typical fizzy lager most often consumed in the United States is only about 5.2%.

And such a powerful beer for the monks is actually not uncommon. Historians determined that an 11th century recipe written by monks for brewing—still in England but at a different monastery—also yielded an ale of at least 12% alcohol. Understanding this makes the whole argument about only drinking beer because they had to a bit shaky, doesn't it?

Many of the Church leaders during this time were known through narratives about beer. St. Arnuf of Austria (580 AD), for example, was said to have ended a plague by dipping his crucifix into a brew kettle and then serving the beer. While far-fetched, as earlier pointed out, monasteries took it upon themselves to care for public health, and one of those methods was to make and serve beer, even to educate the public about drinking beer instead of water.

Similarly, Arnold of Soissons of the Abbey of St. Peter in the late 11th century insisted people drink beer not water for their health. Obviously he was a popular guy. And, of course, he was carrying out the Church's mission to serve the people (even if he was serving them beer).

During the Middle Ages we also get the oldest reference to hops in brewing, which was made by an Abbot. Specifically it was made by the Abbot Adalhard of Corbie in 822. It wasn't an admission to hopping all of their ale (making beer, in other words) but rather a reference to it as an ingredient in a recipe.

In contrast to this Abbot's use of hops, however, St. Hildegard of Bingen campaigned strongly during the 12th century against hops in beer, blaming it for the affliction "brewer's droop," among other maladies.

Hildegard wasn't alone in her dislike of hops. In the 13th century, the Bishop of Cologne tried to get hopped beer banned, but primarily because it competed with the church's own ale recipes. The church at the time was also the only source for gruit, which it sold to other brewers. And so if hops became popular the Church would be out a lot of money.

Eventually, though, hops became valuable. Saint Wenceslas (907-935 AD) actually ordered the death penalty for anyone caught exporting beer hops from Belgium because he didn't want outsiders to compete with the Belgium brewers. Actually, it could be argued that in certain places they were already valuable. In the mid 9th century at the monasteries of St. Remi, Lobbes and St. Germain tenants had to pay their rent in hops.

Beer was a popular beverage in the Middle Ages, throughout Europe and for all occasions. In 1237 the Archbishop of Trondheim (Norway) asked in a letter to Pope Gregory IX if beer could be used at mass instead of wine. This can be explained of course, because in Norway perhaps it was too difficult to grow their own wine and so they had to purchase it from elsewhere: an expensive alternative. We have no record of the Pope's response, so don't know how it turned out.

However we do know that in 1241 Pope Gregory IX told Archbishop Trondhjem of Norway in a letter that he could *no longer* Baptize people with beer.

But then, almost as payback in the 13th century, Polish King Leszek the White (or Leszek the I) told Pope Honorius III in a letter that he couldn't crusade. He stated that he was so sick he could only take beer or mead, and since there was none to be had on the crusades he and his soldiers would stay put. We can't really blame him all that much.

Beer wasn't all that the monks contributed to in the Middle Ages, though. Liqueurs (think Frangelico) were made in Italy as far back as the 13th century, most often by monks of various orders.

And some, meanwhile, were really into their wine. The 12th century Cistercian monks of Burgundy, for example, literally tasted the soil to determine the best place to plant wine grapes. The region, of course, has become famous for its grapes and wine production. Tasting the soil, apparently, makes a difference.

Finally to wrap up this period, and especially the Church's involvement in it, think of this narrative. According to legend, in 988 AD the Grand Prince of Kiev wanted to convert to a religion for political purposes. He invited Jews to discuss their religion. While impressed, he wasn't sold because the Jews had no land for themselves.

Then he asked the Muslims to present their religion and was again impressed but decided not to convert because Muslims couldn't drink. Finally, the Catholic Church made an appeal, and confirmed that he and his people would be able to imbibe as much as they wanted should they decide to be Catholics.

Therefore, because he was still able to drink, the Grand Prince and his people converted to Christianity. The rest is history.

The Renaissance

(1300-1699)

The Renaissance was a worldwide cultural movement that saw the spread of new and innovative forms of literature, diplomacy, science, and education. During this same time there was also a renaissance in alcoholic beverages and the drinking culture.

Innovations in brewing, fermenting, distilling, and winemaking all changed the course of history and society. At the same time mankind started viewing drinking and alcoholic beverages in new ways.

Distilled beverages, beer, wine, fermented drinks of all kinds all became commodities. They became integral parts of economies, items of trade, export and import. They funded wars, caused riots, established laws and set up power structures.

Creating these drinks became commercialized and then later industrialized. To aid these ventures we see some of the most important inventions of the time. We also see opportunist entrepreneurs, merchants and whole classes of people become wildly rich off of supplying booze to a thirsty people.

Certain drinks become defined, create an identity, and then claim a foothold in their respective geographic locales. Now, whole countries are known for the drinks they produce rather than anything else.

In short we enter a third phase in the evolution of alcoholic beverages and civilization's changing drinking culture. We enter a period that, along with the rest, helps us understand where we came from and where we're going.

Explorers and Pirates

It was in the Renaissance period that mankind really began looking outward. From all over Europe, explorers started wondering what was over the next hill, the next mountain, or the ocean. Alcohol, of course, played a big part in the exploration of new worlds. And it played a part in many different ways.

Alcohol was a provision on these journeys, either to help boost the health of the men and women that went along, or as an incentive to go in the first place. It was the reason that many expeditions were shaped in the form we now know them in. It was also the catalyst for survival in many episodes.

When Magellan, arguably one of the most notable explorers in history, prepared for his voyage around the world in 1519 he spent more money on sherry than on weapons. We don't think he underestimated the danger he would face. However he knew perfectly well that alcohol would be valuable on the high seas.

Not too long after Magellen's adventure Sir Francis Drake was exploring the world, and exploring new drinks. In fact, the mojito traces its origins to a cocktail called El Draque, first mixed in Cuba in 1586 for Sir Francis Drake's men during his expedition.

According to his accounts his men were weak from lack of nutrition, and so South American Indians mixed what has come to be known as the first cocktail. The ingredients they used were aguardiente de cana (a kind of crude rum), dissolved bark extract from the chuchuhuasi tree, limes, mint and sugarcane juice. The drink nursed Drake's men back to health and they were on their way.

El Draque (oldest cocktail) Recipe

2 ounces Rum

6 Mint Leaves

2 tsp Sugar

1 Lime

Drop a few leaves of mint in a short glass.

Cut the lime in 8 pieces. Drop all pieces in the glass.

Add the sugar.

Muddle the lime pieces with a wooden spoon. This will also bruise the mint leaves.

Add a few ice cubes.

Top with rum.

Historians also credit the discovery of lager beer (like Coors or Budweiser) to yet another famous explorer, Christopher Columbus.

Lager was discovered in a German monastery in the 15th century. However, the yeast that makes lager possible is not native to Germany, or to Europe for that matter. In fact scientists have traced it to the Beachwood forests of South America. It could have been possible that Columbus stopped near these forests during his first expedition, and brought wood back (with the yeast on it) that somehow ended up at that monastery.

Speaking of Christopher Columbus, he mentions as a reason for making land in the new world the fact that they were running low on beer. He met native peoples who drank a form of beer made from corn.

His need to make land when the beer was running out is understandable considering in the 16th century English sailors received a ration of one gallon of beer per day and soldiers received two-thirds of a gallon. Beer was often safer to drink than water on long voyages because the water (typically bad to begin with) would spoil and sour.

Rum was also being perfected about this time in the Caribbean. And, as in the movies, pirates loved this drink. In fact there was a certain Captain Henry Morgan, who raided Spanish settlements in the Caribbean in late 1680s who was known to love the stuff. The brand of rum, Captain Morgan Spiced Rum, was named after him.

At the same time in Mexico, mid-16th century Spanish conquistadors ran out of the brandy they had brought on their voyage so they looked to create a liquor out of the indigenous plants.

Pirates smuggling rum, 1600s.

They finally settled on the agave plant and first roasted it, then crushed it to get its sweet juice, and then finally distilled it into a spirit. What these explorers gave us was tequila, born of necessity.

This new drink would come to be very popular in its native land. In 1600, Don Pedro Sanchez de Tagle began mass-producing tequila at the first dedicated distillery for it in the territory of modern-day Jalisco, Mexico.

Drunken history was also being made in other parts of the Americas as well.

Before carrying the pilgrims to the new world in 1620 the Mayflower was a merchant vessel that primarily carried wine from France and Spain to England (almost fitting somehow).

In fact, between 1609 and 1620 there were only two journeys the Mayflower made that didn't involve hauling wine. Once it had deposited its load of settlers at Plymouth, the Mayflower then went back to doing what it did best.

Ironically the Pilgrims finally did land at Plymouth because they were dangerously low on beer and couldn't go any further. In fact the diary of one of the Mayflower's passengers reads, "We could not now take time for further search...our victuals being much spent, especially our beer..." As mentioned before, the ship's water supply was probably dank and dangerous to drink.

Following in the footsteps of the first pilgrims, English Puritans sailed for Boston on April 8, 1630. Their ship, the Arbella, was carrying 10,000 gallons of wine and 10,584 gallons of beer (3 times more beer than water) according to the ship's log.

New England had by this time been settled for 10 years and was getting supplies from England on an occasional basis. One such supply ship, the British ship Talbot, arrived in 1629 with five tons of beer and 20 gallons of brandy. Definitely the necessities.

America's Pioneers, Pilgrims and Settlers

The exploration and the colonizing of the new world was of course a highlight of this period. America had people from every great European power in the world on her shores, and all of them brought their unique tastes and cultures. These tastes, of course, included a thirst for certain types of beverages.

There is also today a persistent belief that because many of the colonists were Puritans, Quakers or other types of strict protestant religions, they were free from partaking in fermented beverages. This belief is, of course, completely false.

In fact, the Puritans and other colonists drank—like anyone else at the time—an immense amount of ale, brandy and wine. Almost as soon as their feet hit dry land they began searching for ways to make these types of drinks again. The same goes for all other colonies as well. America, was founded, so to speak, on drink!

In 1587 at Sir Walter Raleigh's Virginia colony settlers brewed their own beer with corn. They apparently didn't like it very much because then corresponded with England asking for ale from home (which was delivered to them in 1607).

However, later Virginia colonists set up a small brewery making maize-beer in 1620. Governor George Thorpe seemed to have liked this batch, writing that "it was a good drink, much preferable to English beer." Maybe a different recipe?

In 1612 the first brewhouse in America was opened, called Block and Christiansen's, in what was then New Amsterdam (now Manhattan). And in 1614 the first non-native American was born in the brewhouse. His name was Jean Vigne and he grew up to become a brewer himself.

Diaries and other artifacts demonstrate that during this period—in the early 1600's—Puritans drank beer throughout the day, from breakfast until they retired to bed. In fact, small beer—beer with about half as much alcohol—was given to children "as soon as they were weaned."

Beer wasn't all there was though. According to letters written to his brother, George Thorpe, a preacher, discovered he could distill spirits with a mash of native corn in Virginia in the 1620s. This of course would eventually lead to the All-American spirit, Bourbon.

In 1622, perhaps in response to Thorpe's discovery the Virginia Company complained to London that the colonists' fondness for alcohol would make them unproductive. As it turned out, they were wrong, but this was the start of a growing temperance sentiment.

Up the coast, to support plans for long-term brewing, the Massachusetts Bay Colony ordered hop seeds from England in 1629.

They could have just talked to their neighbors to the south though. New York began producing hops in 1629 and then commercially in 1630, and New York eventually became the main source of hops for beer in America, growing 3 million pounds by 1855.

In the same year (1629), maybe looking for variety, the Massachusetts Bay colonists also planted their first apple orchard. Not for food, but—according to historical documents—so they could make alcoholic cider.

A year later (in 1630) in the southwestern part of the continent—what is now Socorro, New Mexico in fact—the first wine grapes planted in the western United States were put in the ground by Spanish missionaries. Vines in the west would dominate the wine industry almost 400 years later.

Finally, after almost 50 years of colonization, the first commercial brewery in America was opened in 1632 in what is now lower Manhattan.

Then, two years later in 1634, the colony at Plymouth (the Pilgrims) licensed the first official tavern for the colony. This represents the start of regulation for businesses selling alcohol.

Not long after the first tavern, in 1636, John Harvard established his college in New England. His plans included something essential for education: a brewhouse—not that uncommon considering students would house themselves there while attending.

However, just three years later, in1639, Harvard president Nathaniel Eaton apparently lost his job because he didn't supply the students with enough beer.

About this time we also start seeing the first legislation concerning beer. In 1637 the legislature of the Massachusetts Bay Colony set the price of beer as "not more than one penny a quart at the most." This was apparently done to ensure colonists had enough on hand to drink and become healthy. Remember, they didn't trust the water, not even in America.

Speaking of legislation, in 1639 Connecticut Governor John Winthrop banned the practice of toasting in the colony's taverns because many believed it led to drunkenness. After all, one could not leave if someone toasted him. Then, that person was obliged to offer a toast in return.

On a lighter note, the first distillery in New York City was built on Staten Island by Dutch settlers the following year (1640). It most likely produced Apple Jack, a drink popular in the area at the time. It was made by distilling hard cider (apples were plentiful at the

Beer for breakfast in Colonial America.

time), either through conventional methods or by freezing it and removing the water that separates from the alcohol.

Although progressive enough to open a distillery, New Amsterdam still had its difficulties. In 1644 the Governor placed a tax on beer to raise money. As a response many brewers refused to pay, which led to a seizure of their beer by the Governor's soldiers.

Not long after, in 1651, Puritans passed the first beer quality laws in America, which specified how much barley taverns should brew with. The reasoning behind this was to ensure quality ale because they wanted people to drink less spirits or wine. If the beer is good, they figured, then that's what people would be more willing to drink.

Another alcohol-related law was passed in 1654, when the Colony of Connecticut banned rum because it was so cheap and easily bought (and of course very potent). This law against rum is actually the first written reference to its name, in all likelihood naming the spirit from then on.

Yet another interesting law was passed in 1656 when Massachusetts decreed that every town in the colony must have a tavern or the citizens would face a fine. Taverns were essentially the public meeting houses for the villages, and would serve as the court or legislative meeting place. It was also typically where mail was delivered, and towns weren't officially recognized as towns until they had a tavern in them.

A year later (1657), however, Massachusetts followed Connecticut's lead and also banned rum from the colony (and of course from the tavern in each town).

Throughout the colonies, though, beer was still a popular beverage. In 1660 New Amsterdam (New York City) had a population of only 1500, but they already had 26 breweries and taverns.

Colonists were proud of their ale, too. In 1662 Massachusetts Governor John Winthrop Jr. travelled to England where the Royal Society of London asked him to present on the novelties of the Americas. He chose to present on the methods of brewing beer with the corn native to the new colonies.

But then, in 1667 the Massachusetts colonists apparently had a change of heart about rum because not only did they lift the previously imposed ban, but they also built the first commercial U.S. rum distillery in Boston that year.

At the end of that decade, in 1669, New Hampshire began legislating alcohol sales. They issued the first license to sell beer to tavern owner Samuel Wentworth. Perhaps coincidentally his son would later become Governor of New Hampshire.

Down the coast, in 1675, Quaker John Fenwick established Fenwick's Colony in Salem, New Jersey. As soon as his followers landed, Fenwick noted in his diary, that they "'busied themselves erecting breweries for manufacturing beer for common drink."

A similar story was found in 1682, when William Penn established the town of Philadelphia. One of his first official acts was to appoint Philadelphia's very first brewmaster.

And settlers to the north were also getting established. In 1668 French colonists built the first commercial brewery in Canada in the town of Quebec (though this was 60 years after the city was founded, which makes one wonder why they took so long).

The period in the new world ends with all of the important elements needed to create a new land: taverns, beer, spirits and the unfortunate laws put in place to regulate them.

Renaissance in the Old World

Changes weren't only occurring in the new world. Europe—the wellspring and source of the Renaissance movement—had more than its share of changes and innovation.

While in America the new inhabitants struggled to simply find or create something resembling the kind of drink they used to have, in Europe we see experimentation with new ingredients and processes. We also see new mechanisms for making alcohol, and new outlooks on drinking and the drinking culture.

We here see much more attention paid to alcohol by the ruling class. It was recognized for its money-generating potential, either through tariffs, taxes, or sales. Alcohol, in all its forms, was worth more than it ever had been before.

With this change came a wealth of other changes related to it. Now those with the knowledge of creating beverages were also worth more. Making these drinks became a craft, which meant it could be protected, refined and perfected.

In short, in Europe we see the very essence of a renaissance in distilling, brewing and winemaking.

In 1500 the German physician and pharmacologist, Hieronymus Brunschwygk, wrote "*Liber de arte distillandi simplicia et composite*" also known as the Little Book of Distilling. This was one of the earliest—if not the first—known book on distillation. While his focus was on the medicinal uses of alcohol and how to make it, his techniques and associated information on ingredients and preparation easily transferred to distilling for consumption.

Around the same time we see another chemist, or alchemist—Paracelsus—working with these "medicinals." He in fact coins the term "alcohol" in the 1500s after combining the Arabic words, alcool and vini meaning "finely divided".

Prior to the 16th century and Brunschwgk's book, and because people thought distilled spirits were mainly used for medicinal purposes, they weren't really popular with the general public. The seeds of change were planted in the 15th century though. Alcohol finally started becoming more common because of its widespread use as medicine during the plague.

The plague was also the cause of one of the most iconic symbols of beer-drinking: the German beer stein with its flip-up lids. Beer steins have those lids because of a 15th century German law requiring all food and beverage containers be covered. The law was made as a method to keep the plague from spreading.

Speaking of Germany, on April 23, 1516, Bavaria passed the *Reinheitsgebot,* or the German Beer Purity Law. This law—applied throughout the German states—stated beer could only be produced with water, barley and hops. It was passed in part to stop competition with bakers for barley. Bakers in this case could solely use rye and other ingredients.

They loved beer in Bavaria during this time. In fact, historians estimate that during the 14th century, alcohol consumption (primarily beer) in Bavaria was almost 80 gallons per year per person.

And according to historical tax documents, the city of Hamburg, with over 600 breweries produced over 5.2 million gallons of beer in the year 1500.

However not all was consumed by people within those towns. Beer was one of the first commodities exported from Germany, sometimes all over the world. In fact the most popular beer of the time was a beer called, Einbeck, first brewed in the town of the same name in 1325 and exported throughout Europe and even as far away as Jerusalem.

Large-scale brewing is commercialized in Europe.

Some beers were so special, though, they were reserved for special occasions. In the 14th century Bock beer, a very strong kind of lager, was only brewed for Easter, Christmas and Lent.

There is little doubt that in Bavaria, beer was king. After all, it made sense from an economics point of view. For example from 1590 to 1620 in Nuremberg one liter of wine cost as much as 6.1 liters of beer.

And as with any other culinary delight, there was found variety. In 1575 Heinrich Knaust wrote a book detailing the types of beer found in Germany and lists *150* different kinds.

But Germany was not the only region crazy about brew. In the city of Amsterdam, for example, there were no less than 126 breweries in 1376. As in the case of Germany they exported throughout Europe.

And historians estimate the per capita beer consumption in Holland in 1600 ranged from 106-159 gallons per year, per person.

In fact, in the 1600s Holland financed its war with Spain almost entirely from taxes collected on beer. Spain in contrast taxed gold (as was tradition) and almost went broke.

Like other countries, Holland was innovating for the purpose of brewing. Dutch scientist Anton van Leeuwenhoek invented the modern microscope in the 1670s, and one of his first observations was beer yeast.

Meanwhile, England was still struggling with the introduction (mainly from Holland) of hopped beer that competed directly to the traditional ale English brewers made. In 1471, in fact, Norwich, England banned the use of hops in brewing.

The people of Norwich weren't alone, either. In 1519 the town of Shrewsbury England banned the use of hops also, calling it a "wicked and pernicious weed."

These sentiments remained all the way through 1651, when the English poet John Taylor called hopped beer, a "Dutch boorish liquor... a saucy intruder."

To fight back against this intruder, brewers organized guilds. One of the earliest brewing organizations in England, the Brewer's Guild, was formed in the 1380s in a London church. Generally this was formed to protect the craft and included only men. Prior to the 1300s it was more common to see women making the beer. In fact, even during the 1400s breweress Margery Kempe was one of the largest suppliers of beer for Henry IV at King's Lynn, England.

Hops, the hated plant that caused brewer's droop.

But then in 1438 we see the first *formal* English brewer's guild, which was established specifically to protect ale brewers (mostly English men) from the invasion of hopped beer (brewed mostly by transplants from elsewhere).

They took their craft—and their use of gruit instead of hops—seriously. In the 1500s if you wanted to brew beer in England you joined this guild and took an oath to "make good and wholesome beer for the man's body." A simple indication that they didn't believe hops to be good or wholesome.

Their attempts to stop the hop didn't work though. As early as 1372, people were finding a taste for hopped beer versus ale. That was the year of the first recorded purchase of hopped beer in London by a Henry Vandale who purchased 4 barrels of the stuff.

It was hard to fight against something so established across the rest of Europe though. In fact one of Sweden's biggest exports during that time was hops, accounting for 14% of total exports for the kingdom in 1491.

In any case, hopped beer caught on as it would in England and the English remained a beer-loving people. Proof is seen in the 16th century in Coventry England, where people consumed an average of 17 pints of ale and beer per week.

Likewise in London during the 14th century, for every 50 residents there was an alehouse which sold ale for only 1 penny per gallon (you can still find some of those places today by the way, like the Blue Anchor in Helston, Cornwall, England that was founded in 1400 and is purported to be the oldest brewpub in Britain).

These alehouses are considered the first *true* bar because they only sold beer, no food or rooms, and they became especially common after the Protestant reformation (1537) closed the monastic breweries.

London was actually considered the beer brewing capital of England at that time. In the year 1572 alone it exported 435,000 gallons of beer to the rest of the country.

Beer was so much a part of the English culture, in fact that there were laws protecting people's supply of it. In 1316 London put price controls on beer, and set stiff penalties for anyone trying to gouge consumers.

And in Scotland, James III (1451-1488) declared a punishment by death for all who "corrupt or mix" wine or beer.

Another demonstration of beer's importance to them is its presence in every place, ritual or event. During Guy Fawkes' Day for example, the day where many Halloween traditions stem from, door to door visitors demanded and got cakes and *beer*, not candy.

Further, in Oxford during the 16th century, brewing and malting were the most popular trades for people to get into.

It was also a common topic of literature. In 1641 Englishman Henry Overton published "Warme Beere" to spread his belief that heated beer was healthier than cold beer.

And In 1615 Gervase Markham pens "The English Huswife," a book containing all of the knowledge a wife of that time should know, including a very detailed recipe for making strong March beer.

We also see some beer-related innovation come from England during this period. For example, in the late 16th century, Alexander Nowell took a bottle of beer with him to fish the Thames. When he opened it, he noticed how fresh it still was. This was the first record of beer in bottles and could have led to the bottle's rising popularity at that time. Alexander Nowell by the way was a puritan and Dean of St. Paul's during Elizabeth I's reign.

As is always the case, the ruling class realized the potential money that could be raised through tariffs on beer. They passed the first set of taxes in 1690, however they were unpopular and people refused to pay them and so they eventually failed. But then in the early 1700s England placed high tariffs on French beverages, like wine and brandy, and then beer taxes became their number one source of revenue.

First distillation through pot still.

The English did like other drinks besides beer and ale, though. For example, the "Humpty Dumpty" in the nursery rhyme referred to a drink of brandy boiled with ale in the 17th century.

And in 1651 the British author, Richard Ligon, pens one of the earliest reviews of rum after visiting Cuba. He didn't seem to care for it, calling it, "a hot, hellish and terrible liquor."

Some would say the English liked to drink too much. In 1644 Oliver Cromwell—ruling as the Lord Protector of England during the Reformation—had Christmas banned in England, largely because of the amount of alcohol (of all kinds) consumed during the holiday.

These different spirits were often from neighboring regions, and were also popular in England, like Irish and Scotch whiskies.

The first written mention of *Irish* whiskey is found during this period, specifically from a 15th century Irish text stating that a chieftain's death was from drinking too much of it.

Likewise the first mention of Scotch whisky was made in a 1494 treasury roll that recorded the transfer of malt by the order of the King to a friar John Cor, "wherewith to make aqua vitae." Aqua vitae—Latin for "water of life"—was the term used for whiskey at the time.

This stuff, too, was taxed by the government. On Christmas day in 1661 the English put a tax on Irish whiskey of 4 pence per gallon. By 1815 it had grown to 6 shillings. Not much of a Christmas present, but it informs us of the drink's popularity and growth.

Brandy, though, was still the spirit of choice. The problem for England was that it was mainly imported from France, their enemy. So in 1690, England passed a law to encourage the distillation of brandy and spirits from corn, something that was cheap and easy to acquire. The hope was the native spirits would prove more popular than the French.

It didn't work; French brandy was as popular as ever. In fact it was the basis for one of the earliest drinking games, called Snapdragon. Brandy and raisins were poured into a shallow bowl, which was then lit on fire. Every person sitting around the bowl had to snatch a flaming raisin out and pop it into their mouth.

Also popular was French champagne. So popular, in fact, that it was during this period the English invented the glass we still use today to quaff down our bubbly. The champagne coupe was designed in 1663 in England specifically for champagne. It was always rumored to be modeled after a woman's breast, but history reveals its shape allows the bubbles to surface and improves the taste of the champagne.

The French, for their part, repaid us by making popular a term we also still use today. The word, "imbibe" gained use in the 14th century as a term used to mean consuming alcohol. It is from the French word, "imbiber," which means "to soak into" (which somehow seems fitting).

The English, by contrast, gave us the phrase, "hair of the dog," as a remedy to cure a hangover in the 16th century. There was an old (at *that* time) belief that you could cure a rabid dog bite by literally putting the dog's hair in the wound.

It was during this period of history the French also improved on something so simple, it's hard to think of life before it: the cork. Corks weren't used in wine bottles until the late 17th century. Before that wine-makers used oil-soaked rags stuffed into the ends of the bottles and sometimes dipped in wax as seals.

For all their innovations, though, the French apparently didn't take too kindly to *over*-imbibing. If you were found drunk in Paris in 1536 you'd be imprisoned and given only bread and water for the first offense, and then whipped for any recurrences.

Lastly of importance to note during this period is the first written reference to the spirit of all spirits: vodka, which was originally thought of as a medicinal (as most spirits were). In his 1534 work on herbs and medicines, physician Stefan Falimierz said that vodka could, "increase fertility and awaken lust." His theory has certainly been proven over the years.

Only six years later, in 1540, Ivan the Terrible monopolized the vodka industry and declared only the monarchy could be licensed distillers. This decree was relaxed a bit later to include the richer classes, but vodka from that point forward became very controlled by the state.

The Church and the Royalty

While during the Renaissance we see private-enterprises increasing their presence in the trade and creation of fermented and distilled beverages, we still see the Church and the various governments involved as well.

Much of the major innovations have taken place. The Church has moved brewing from the kitchen to large-scale productions. All that's left to do now is refine the process and create new variations.

However, we still see the Church creating new and important drinks that are common today. In addition, we see evidence of the church—and the government—trying to control how society enjoyed their drinks. We begin seeing more regulation, more laws and more edicts. But, on the flip side, we also see a growing popularity of whiskey.

In 1300 AD Scottish monastic infirmaries would often give patients whiskey to treat smallpox, colic and palsy. It never really cured them, but the patients were happy.

After the monasteries were closed during the Protestant Reformation, though, the monks who had previously been the monastic distillers found new jobs, either teaching others to distill or opening their own distilleries.

And so in 1505 the very first license to produce and sell Scotch whisky was given to the Guild of Surgeon Barbers in Edinburgh by James IV.

Only a year later in 1506, treasury rolls in the Scottish town of Dundee record that the local barber was paid to provide "aqua vitae for the king's pleasure." Apparently the King was a fan. Notice also that by now just about all pretext of whiskey being used for medicine has been dropped.

As it turns out the Scottish had a legacy of appreciating whiskey (and other drinks). In 1589 King James VI of Scotland gave Anne of Norway a Quaich—a traditional Scottish cup used for drinking fermented or distilled beverages—to show his love.

But once the church was back in England in the mid-1600s, it didn't seem to like the fact that others were distilling for the public. In fact, in 1655 distiller Robert Haig was censured by the Church for operating a still on the Sabbath. For shame. This was, however, the first reference to a commercial still.

Not too far away, another innovation was taking place: the creation of gin. The English were first introduced to this spirit When William III, a Dutchman, ascended the English throne in 1689. He quickly declared gin the preferred drink of the court.

First produced in Holland in the 1600s by the Dutch physician Franciscus Sylvius, gin was initially a medicine for stomach problems, gout and gallstones.

Yet another new drink was being introduced in France: sparkling wine. Though most people think of Dom Pergnon as its inventor, the oldest recorded sparkling wine is Blanquette de Limoux, invented by Benedictine Monks in the Abbey of Saint Hilaire in 1531.

Dom Perignon, however, while not the inventor of champagne, was a Benedictine monk who worked as cellar master in an abbey in the 17th and 18th centuries. He actually *is* credited for inventing the "basket" that fits around the cork on a champagne bottle, still an important creation.

Yet another monk would give us the recipe for one of the most popular spirits today. The first recipe for Russian vodka was written in 1430 by a monk named Isidore from a Moscow monastery (though the first written reference would come 100 years later). Talk about a contribution.

Most monasteries at this time were also still brewing, just not as much as they did in the Middle Ages because they were no longer the commercial source for beer and ale in the community.

The Trappist monastic order was founded in France in 1664, and the first Trappist brewery opened just 21 years later in 1685.

And in 1677 the Reutberg Cloisters (Germany) got approval to brew beer especially for the sisters working all day in the fields. This brewery still exists.

The Paulaner monks moved from Italy and began brewing Doppelbock beer in the late 17th century in Germany. They named it "Salvator" (Savior) and it was one of their most cherished varieties. Again,

Drunken tavern scene. Not much changed.

this is still made today.

It's not an exaggeration to say the church was soaked in beer. Polish legend says that when Pope Clement VIII (Pope during the 17th century) became very sick and weak, he asked for "*piva di Varva,*" meaning beer from Warka, Poland.

Many of these beers were the lager-style, but during this time England was beginning to create new forms as well. For example the first written use of the term "stout" as a beer variety is found in this period (1677), used by the Earl of Bridgewater while talking about a kind of strong beer being made. Even more varieties are created over the next 200 years.

From this period we also get an accounting of the appetite those in the church and the ruling class had for drink. Like William Wareham who was made archbishop of Canterbury in 1504. At the banquet held for him to celebrate being made Archbishop, guests went through 5400 gallons of beer and ale.

Only 38 years later, in 1542, records show that Henry VIII's Hampton Court Palace was consuming over 13,000 pints of ale and beer every day. Every single day!

And while residing in Avignon France in the 1300s the Pope and his entourage consumed over 2,600 gallons of wine per week.

Beer was also needed on the front lines. In 1418 the city of London sent 75,000 gallons of beer and 50,000 gallons of ale to Henry V while he was campaigning in France. There was no way for either of them to stay good more than a few weeks or a couple of months, so it must have all been consumed by his men in a short time. That's a good leader!

The Revolution

(1700-1799)

Revolution can be defined as a fundamental change in power or organizational structures, or a sudden, complete or marked change in something. In the brief 100 years we cover in this chapter that's exactly what we see: a world that's changed drastically in a number of ways.

In the Americas, revolution was in the making, and then eventually occurred. Taverns and pubs were where the revolution was conceived and planned. They were where the founders created a new nation and discussed the ideals and considerations for making it.

Drink was consumed and sold to fuel the revolution. It warmed the hearts and spirits of the men fighting and was responsible for many of the victories.

The men who created this country were also integrally bound to distilling or fermenting. They were connoisseurs or makers of booze, and their lives often somehow revolved around alcohol. When the dust settled, many of their lives after the revolution continued to somehow be affected by drink.

There wasn't only the American Revolution during this period either, there were actually fundamental changes taking place around the globe. In terms of drink—of making it, of consuming it, and of selling it—revolution is the key word to use.

Alcohol touched mankind during all of this upheaval and all of these new stages. It helped shape the revolutions, and also helped determine their ends.

Shots Heard 'Round the World

America was busy between 1700 and 1799. There was the obvious period of the revolution, but it was much more than that. The people of the time were creating not only a new country but a new identity, right down to what they drank. New drinks became popular, and others were born, all from local ingredients and through the innovation of the people who moved here.

We also see the start of full-fledge commercial enterprises as they relate to alcohol, whether brewing or distilling. The trend of liquor and beer as commodities was realized like never before, and many became wealthy or at the very least significantly improved their stations as a result.

More than any other period in our history, we also have a firm grasp on how much people of the time drank, and the numbers are staggering (no pun intended).

Americans loved their drink. It is estimated that by 1700 in the Americas aclcohol consumption totaled over 10 gallons per year per capita. A lot by any measurement, but considering today it is just about half of that in alcohol total (beer and liquor).

One of the main causes was the cheap price of easily bought rum. A popular expression in the late 1700s for describing someone who was drunk was, "he's been to Barbados." Barbados was the main supplier of rum at the time.

That changed, however as rum distilleries were set up in the colonies, the first in Boston. The manufacture of rum became early Colonial New England's biggest and most prosperous industry.

And in the late 1700s New England rum was considered the best. By 1763 Boston and Salem—with a combined population of just over 25,000—had over 60 distillers.

With the influx of new distillers and entrepreneurs selling rum, the cost of course plummeted. In the American colonies in 1673, a gallon of rum cost 6 shillings, but by 1783 it was only 8 pennies per gallon. Cheap enough even for the poorest of people.

To some the plummeting price and readily available spirits created an atmosphere of excess, and perhaps they were right. At 1700s gentlemen dinners servants were on hand to loosen the neckties of those who passed out after eight hours of drinking so they wouldn't suffocate.

This was, after all, the period that gave us hip flasks, small reusable bottles easily concealed in a pocket and originally used by the gentrified classes for carrying a bit of booze around with them. They didn't really become used by the general or mainstream population until during prohibition.

Booze, in other words, was always on hand and always, always consumed.

We also happen to have a number of statistics that tell us how much early Americans were drinking. According to historians, by about 1750 the average American was consuming about four gallons of rum per year. And a statistic from 1770 places the per capita consumption of all distilled spirits at 3.7 gallons per year per adult male. Again, as a manner of comparison, the current statistics for the United States place us at about five gallons of all alcohol combined (spirits, beer and wine) in our current age.

Drunken tavern scene from the 1700s. Still the same…

Again, part of the reason for the mass consumption was the relative small expense of booze. In Philadelphia in 1731, for example, a quart of wine was two shillings, a gill (1/4 pint) of rum was a tuppance, and you'd only pay three pennies for a quart of beer.

And just about every occasion was an occasion to imbibe. The day a minister was ordained, for example, was big in the American colonies and taverns would even brew special "ordination" ales for the event. At one particularly festive ordination in New England in 1785, 68 people drank 18 bottles of wine 8 bottles of brandy and 44 bowls of rum punch—a popular drink at the time made with rum, sugar and fruit juices.

Rum aside, American colonists were also crazy about their beer. John Adams once stated in a letter written when he was a 15 year old student at Harvard that his breakfasts consisted of bread and beer. It was, in short, everywhere.

Many early Americans climbed the social ladder through brewing. Like Mary Lisle, the first female American commercial brewer who ran the Edinburgh Brewhouse in Philadelphia from 1734-1751.

Or John Barnitz, who opened the first brewery in Baltimore—which as it turns out was also the first manufacturing industry in Baltimore—in 1748. A year later Barnitz died, but his son then ran it until 1780. The spot where the brewery sat was used to make beer for the next 200 years.

Brewers like Lisle and Barnitz came to be *revered* in the community, especially by those who worried about the increased consumption of rum. In 1792 New Hampshire exempted breweries from property taxes because beer "...diminishes the use of spirits and promotes health." In other words they wanted to give brewers an edge over rum or gin.

Though that's not to say that people didn't enjoy drinking beer all the time already. Just look at Reading, Pennsylvania, which in 1760 with a population of only about 2000 people had over 30 taverns. Brewing, in fact, was one of Reading's biggest industries.

Martha Washington's Rum Punch

This is actually the recipe that Martha Washington used to make rum punch for her household's parties.

3 oz. White Rum
3 oz. Dark Rum
3 oz. Orange Curacao
4 oz. Simple Syrup
4 oz. Lemon Juice
4 oz. Fresh Orange Juice
3 Lemons quartered
1 Orange quartered
1/2 Tsp. Grated nutmeg
3 Cinnamon sticks (broken)
6 Cloves
12 oz. Boiling water

In a container, mash the orange, lemons, cinnamon sticks, cloves and nutmeg. Add syrup, lemon and orange juice. Pour the boiling water over the mixture in a container. Let it cool for a few minutes then add the white rum, dark rum and orange curaco. Strain well into a pitcher or punch bowl and serve over ice in goblets and decorate with wheels of lemon and orange. Dust with a little nutmeg and cinnamon.

Beer was so popular that anything and everything was used to brew with. The Ben Franklin-founded, American Philosophical Society published the earliest recipe for pumpkin ale in 1771. This was nothing like the spiced-beers of today, but a simple beer with a slight melon flavor. Yet pumpkins were plentiful, so it made sense to use them.

And even the strict James Oglethorpe, after landing in Georgia with settlers in 1733, had a brewery built on Jekyll Island by 1738.

Oglethorpe preferred beer to rum, but as it turned out he wasn't above rum consumption when used for the right purposes. In 1735 he gave local Indians gifts, which included 8 kegs of rum to get them to sell the land for the Georgia Colony. Ironically, after attributing eight deaths to over-drinking of rum, Oglethorpe convinced the Georgia Colony trustees to ban it for the colonists.

Parliament, however, rescinded the 1735 Georgia ban on rum in 1742 because it simply couldn't be enforced. People charged with enforcing it were actually selling rum on the side.

This was also a time when barkeeps and tavern-owners were seen as highly educated and important members of society. In 1774, for example, there was a Connecticut tavern owner Joel White, who was also the town's Justice of the Peace, the Town Treasurer and the area's State Representative. Even eventual U.S. President Martin Van Buren's father owned a tavern (and, as it happened, Van Buren was born in that tavern).

The taverns themselves were incredibly important to the public, and are the locales for much of the planning for the revolution. The Boston Tea Party, in fact, was organized at the Green Dragon Tavern in Boston, Massachusetts.

Tun Tavern, home of the U.S. Marine Corps.

Similarly the very first United States Marine recruiting station was in a bar. Robert Mullan, owner of The Tun Tavern on the waterfront in Philadelphia, was appointed chief Marine Recruiter by the Continental Congress, and so began getting new Marines on November 10, 1775 in his own bar.

In the military the thirst for drink was as strong as it was in the public. And sometimes just as satiated. All branches had a spirit ration of one kind or another. The spirit ration for the U.S. Army in 1785 was 4 ounces of rum, brandy or whiskey per day (although this was reduced to 2 oz in 1790).

And for the very first warship the new country produced, the USS Constitution, it seemed like its entire mission revolved around alcohol. She first sailed on July 27, 1798, with 79,400 gallons of rum. Only three months later in Jamaica she took on another 68,300 gallons. Two weeks after loading up on rum, she then took on 64,300 gallons of wine.

Then in November of 1798, the USS Constitution captured 12 English merchant ships. The sailors and Marines on board scuttled all of them, plundering only their (you guessed it) rum.

She sailed closer to England in December and January, and on January 26, 1799 her crew raided a Scottish whisky distillery. They sacked the operation and took 40,000 gallons of Scotch aboard the ship. She finally returned home in February, making port on the 20th, with no whisky and 38,600 gallons of *water* left in her hold.

This century was also the century for America's native spirit, rye—and then later corn mash—whiskey. Evan Shelby was the first to set up a distillery in Tennessee (where Jack Daniels is still made). He founded it in 1771 near Holston to produce rye whiskey exclusively.

Years later it was Nashville's turn, getting its first tavern, also a rye whiskey distillery, in 1787 when John Boyd opened the Red Heifer.

As the west expanded so did the distillers, moving from Tennessee just north. In 1783 Evan Williams opened the first commercial distillery in Kentucky, which is the best-known locale in the world for American whiskey. The brand Evan Williams Kentucky Bourbon is still sold today, and is one of the most popular brands of bourbon in the world.

Another master distiller arrived in Kentucky in the early 1780s, Basil Hayden. His whiskey was apparently very notable and extremely popular in the area. He was also responsible for moving the Catholic Church into the territory, giving the land for the first Catholic Church in Kentucky in 1787. Later, his grandson became a distiller and named his whiskey to honor his grandfather. The whiskey is still around today, known as Old Grand-Dad. Jim Beam also currently makes a whiskey in its small-batch line called, Basil Hayden, reportedly using his recipe.

Then, in 1789, the whiskey world changed forever. A certain Baptist minister, Reverend Elijah Craig—also a distiller—was fond of cleaning his whiskey barrels by setting the insides on fire and charring them. According to legend, he charred the inside of some barrels, filled them with corn mash whiskey, and then forgot about them for a couple of years. When he found them and then tried the whiskey, what he drank was a mellow, smoky drink the color of caramel. He had invented American Bourbon whiskey.

The number of distilleries at this time in the United States exploded. In 1792 there were

Father of American whiskey, Elijah Craig.

just over 3000 distilleries, and just 18 years later, in 1810, there were a reported 14,191 distilleries producing a whopping 25.5 million gallons of whiskey per year.

And by this time, our appetites had grown even thirstier. While in 1700 we were drinking about 4 gallons of spirits per year, estimates state that by the 1790s an average American over the age of 15 years old was drinking just under 6 gallons of absolute alcohol each year.

Beer was still very much in demand (in 1791 alone the Pennsylvania Gazette reported that Philadelphia merchants received 20 *tons* of hops from Boston that year) but we were increasingly turning to the native spirits.

In 1792 Kentucky was admitted to the Union, and almost immediately its two biggest exports were hemp and bourbon whiskey, both of which they'd put on the nearby Ohio River to send to the rest of the country.

From there, enterprising distillers took their craft to other cities and regions. Cleveland, Ohio, established in 1796, had its first distillery in 1800 making 2 quarts of raw spirits per day.

In 1799 there were less than 4,000 residents of Davidson County, Tennessee, but there were already 61 stills making whiskey. Clearly, it was important to the American people.

In fact, capping off this century, we see the first violent protest in the new United States occurring in 1794 when the government placed an excise tax on whiskey. Grain farmers who typically turned surplus grains into whiskey to sell were hit with the tax especially hard.

In July of that year more than 500 farmers and rebels marched on the home of a local tax collector in Western Pennsylvania. The Federal Government—George Washington, in fact—responded by raising and sending a militia of 15,000 men to suppress the uprising. No battles took place, but the episode demonstrates both the importance of distilling to the people producing it, and to the government as a revenue source.

The World and its Revolution

Revolution existed throughout the world during this decade. Here we see a variety of drinks, flavors, and customs taking shape. The Renaissance educated people about better techniques, and they sought higher quality and more effective methods for fermenting or distilling.

People also increased their consumption of these beverages. And why not? As techniques improved so did the product and the quantity available. As seen in the Americas the price also plummeted as a result.

The explosion in variation created new tastes and made for an exciting drinking culture. Whereas before there was the pretext of drinking because the water was contaminated, we now see a culture embracing drinking for drinking's sake.

The beginning of the century found two super-powers, England and France, at war with each-other. And so, war had an effect on what was consumed by drinkers as well as other people. The war with France actually deprived England of wine, which was popular in the court so they turned to Portugal, who fortified their wine with aguardente (distilled wine) to avoid spoilage and at the same time created port wine.

The war with France also created shortages of many supplies in England (and thereby, the Americas). According to English naval journals from 1718, this included supplies on the ships themselves. That year, the Admiral of the Fleet ordered rationing of all ship supplies in the navy. All but beer, that is.

Then in 1730 the British Navy did something that would become tradition. It began a rum ration for all sailors of 1/8 pint per day. The rum was actually stronger than was typically found publically, and was called a "tot". On July 31, 1970 the Royal Navy discontinued this ration, and the day became known as "Black Tot Day."

Another important occasion happened in 1740, when British Vice Admiral Edward Vernon, who wore a coat of grogram cloth, introduced a mix of beer and rum to the sailors to make the ration last longer. The combination wasn't popular and became known as "grog" as a nod to the Vice Admiral.

But for the English, during this period, the most notorious spirit was gin. It was introduced by the Dutch, and dirt cheap to make and buy. In 1743 the English were drinking 2.2 gallons of it per capita annually. That doesn't sound like a lot, but this includes all men, women and children in the country.

The government tried to intervene as best it could to control the waterfall of juniper-laced spirits from the many gin-houses. England's Gin Act of 1736 imposed high taxes on gin retailers, but it wasn't that popular, and people resisted (it actually led to riots in the streets). Eventually it was abolished altogether in 1742.

The proliferation of places to get gin was one of the main problems England was having. In 1740, with a population of just under 500,000, of the 96,000 houses in London, more than 15,000 of them sold alcohol. Of those, 9,000 were gin-shops while the rest sold beer.

The gin consumption of the English finally peaked at 18 million gallons per year in 1743, the most harrowing statistic since gin's introduction, but eventually it dropped to 7 million gallons per year by 1751. The drop was due to a number of factors, including widespread PR campaigns against the drink, and (once again) tariffs and taxes imposed.

Even during the gin-craze, though, England was entering its Golden Age of brewing (realized more formally in the 1800s). Brewers started experimenting with different varieties of flavoring hops (instead of preservative hops) in the mid 1700s. The style they came up with, a combination of three styles of beer (ale, hopped ale, and two-penny beer, or small beer) was named after the brewers' favorite customers, porters.

This was a significant advancement in brewing for a number of reasons. For example, porter was the first beer that was brewery-aged and then sold ready for immediate consumption. Before this style, beer was usually aged at the pub and then sold in open containers (like buckets) to take home for consumption. Porter, however, would pave the road for packaged beer.

It became insanely popular too. In 1748 the largest brewers in London were specializing in porter, with the biggest making over 50,000 barrels that year.

However, the strongest beer in London, by no small measure, was the stout. This was a much more expensive beer to make, and the most expensive to buy, costing 40 shillings— or 170 shillings today—for a barrel (or $274.00 U.S. dollars).

Not only was it more expensive for the larger amount of ingredients, but also for the taxes on those ingredients. England didn't have a true tax on beer, but instead brewers paid taxes on the malt. Those beers—like stouts—that used more malt ended up with a higher price due to the taxes on them.

Gin Row: illustration showing the results of gin in London, 1700s.

The late 18th century also saw more, important innovations in terms of brewing. The first steam engine in London, for example, was installed in the Red Lion porter brewery in 1784. It did the work of dozens of men and proved to be much safer too.

And then in1797 Joseph Bramah invented the first beer pump, which allowed beer to be stored below in a cold cellar. Before this invention, beer barrels were stored above the bar and used gravity to fill mugs. The floors above were often, obviously, warmer than those below, and so beer was not only warmer, but often spoiled much more quickly. These beer pumps were used until the 1960s in most every pub in the country.

Great Britain was also producing massive amounts of distilled spirits, primarily north of England though (and not always shared with the rest of the world). In Scotland, whisky production increased from 100,000 gallons in 1708 to 250,000 gallons in 1736. Interestingly, almost all of it was consumed in Scotland. However, because of high taxes, in 1780 there were only eight legal distilleries in Scotland and 400 illegal—or unlicensed—ones.

Ireland at this time was also seeing a boom in whiskey production. In 1780 there were over 2000 distilleries in Ireland. This was to change, unfortunately: in 1887 there were only 28 distilleries, and today there are only 3 (Midleton, Bushmills and Cooley).

The drop in Irish whisky production was despite its popularity. In the 18th century for example Czar Peter the Great of Russia wrote, "Of all the wines of the world, Irish spirit is the best!"

This despite the fact that at the time Russian, non-state vodka producers would put their vodka through four distillations, and by all accounts it would have been considerably smoother than anything sold today—serious competition for Irish whiskey, but to each his own.

As Peter the Great demonstrates, the end of the century sees a variety of beverage preferences. For example, those who sailed with Captain Cook on his first voyage in 1768 were treated to 250 barrels of beer, 44 barrels of brandy, and 17 barrels of rum. We know all about this variety through the ship's logs. But what we don't know is if they carried what appeared to be the bane of the ruler of Germany—coffee.

In the mid-18th century coffee was being imported into Europe from the Middle East. Popular in Turkey, Spain and other Muslim-controlled or influenced countries it quickly became popular in cafes and salons. In Germany it threatened to overtake beer consumption.

And then in 1777 Frederick the Great of Germany issued an edict telling people to drink beer, and not coffee. He said, "It is disgusting to notice the increase in coffee used by my subjects. My people must drink beer."

There is no record of whether or not this worked, but beer remained safely installed as a staple in Prussia.

To end out the revolutionary century around the world, the French figured out how to open champagne bottles with sabers—sabering, invented by Napoleon's cavalry in the late 1700s—and Spain banned the import of mescal and brandy into California in 1794 (though Californians set up the first still in 1800).

All in all, a time of many changes, new drinks and techniques, and a better world for all of it.

Our Founding Fathers

The most famous characters of this period were closely associated with alcohol and drinking in one form or another. Often, people are surprised at how much our heroes of the time had to do with drink. But drink they did. A lot, and all the time.

In fact, not only did they drink beverages, they made them and sold them as well. Some of our idols, the men whom we learned about in elementary school, were in fact some of the most prolific brewers and distillers of their age.

Benjamin Franklin was not one of those known for drinking in excess. His beverage of choice was wine and he preferred the intellectual stimulation of conversation to drinking. But he appreciated that other people drank. In 1737 Benjamin Franklin had a "Drinker's Dictionary" in his Pennsylvania Gazette listing 228 slang terms for drunkenness in Philadelphia, including such favorites as "His Head is full of Bees," and "Haunted with Evil Spirits."

Franklin did drink beer on a regular basis, but only the weakest of kinds. He had what was called small beer, an unfiltered porridge-like beer with low alcohol content, most every day with his breakfast. At the time small beer was considered healthy and nutritionally valuable, so it wouldn't have seemed that odd. But we *can* say as a result that Ben Franklin liked to have beer most every day of his adult life.

Franklin was also very familiar with the drinking culture of the time. In fact, he wrote in his diary that as an apprentice at the newspaper his duties were interrupted daily to go fetch beer for the other workers. Not uncommon (especially for writers).

And in 1765 when Franklin was living in England, he often noted the drinking habits of the English. He particularly wrote about those working in the London printing shop, saying that during the day workers had at least six pints while working.

Meanwhile in 1757 George Washington ran for the Virginia House of Burgesses. It was his first political campaign and he lost. But then in 1758 Washington ran again, but campaigned differently. At one event he used 160 gallons of rum to treat 391 voters. This time he won by 70 votes. He never lost another political campaign again.

Washington knew he was onto something with the rum. In 1777 he sent his request for rations to the Continental Congress and included a spirit ration for his troops. He stated that it was "essential to the morale of soldiers to have moderate supplies of whiskey." No wonder he's on Mount Rushmore.

Then in 1777 he issued rations of 1/2 gill (1/8 pint) of rum per man per day during the winter at Valley Forge. Not unusual really. But what endeared him to his men was his insistence that the enlisted receive the rum ahead of officers.

He really understood that the simple act of having a drink tapped into something in his troops. In 1778 Washington celebrated Independence Day with an artillery salute and double rations of rum, and his men loved him even more.

Records also demonstrate that Washington himself was a great imbiber. At New York's 1783 Evacuation Day celebration—a drunken romp for the whole city when the British finally left—he chose to party at Sam Fraunces' Tavern. Washington himself made 13 toasts with hot buttered rum. This was the same tavern he frequented before the war—he was actually good friends with the owner—and it is where he bid farewell to his officers and resigned from the army.

Goerge Washington's farewell to his officers in Fraunces Tavern.

And at his inauguration in 1789, Washington insisted on a barrel of Barbados rum for himself and his guests. At the time rum was made in many American coastal towns, and Barbados rum was considered off-limits because it wasn't made in the new U.S. However, it was *also* considered the best.

Once out of office, Washington even began *making* booze. He founded a distillery at his Mount Vernon home in 1797. And in 1799 George Washington, leader of the American Revolution and the first President of the United States, distilled over 11,000 gallons of rye whiskey. He sold almost all of it but saved 150 gallons of it for himself, paying $300 in taxes and making over $7,500—about $200,000 today.

George Washington's Personal Beer Recipe

This recipe was what Washington himself followed to make his beer (directly quoted from his instructions).

To Make Small Beer:

Take a large Siffer full of Bran Hops to your Taste. Boil these 3 hours then strain out 30 Gall into a cooler put in 3 Gall Molasses while the Beer is Scalding hot or rather draw the Melasses into the cooler & Stain the Beer on it while boiling Hot. let this stand till it is little more than Blood warm then put in a quart of Yeat if the Weather is very Cold cover it over with a Blank & let it Work in the Cooler 24 hours then put it into the Cask—leave the bung open till it is almost don Working—Bottle it that day Week it was Brewed."

Yet another Founding Father that appreciated his beverages was Thomas Jefferson. Proof of this is quickly found at his home in Monticello, where even his earliest designs for the property included both a brewing room and a beer cellar.

He eventually built his dedicated brewery later in life, and in the early 1800's began the pursuit of making beer. In the fall of 1820 he brewed three, 60-gallon barrels of ale, much more than had ever been brewed there before (before her death, his wife, Martha regularly brewed 15 gallon batches for the table). Evidence and records from Monticello even suggest Jefferson planted a sizable hop garden as early as 1794.

Perhaps most telling was that among the books at his Monticello library when he died was found one, very worn copy of "The Theory and Practice of Brewing." This book is typically considered the first comprehensive book on brewing by Michael Combrune and was published in 1762.

Whether this affected his view of beer or not isn't known, but we do know that Thomas Jefferson liked stronger beers. He once complained in a letter that because public breweries (pubs or taverns of the day) used a bushel of malt to brew 15 gallons, their beer was "meager" and "vapid." By comparison Jefferson used a bushel for every 8-10 gallons, making a much stronger beer (meaning more alcohol).

Though in truth this "meager-ness" didn't stop Jefferson from drinking what others brewed anyway. When he was Secretary of State (1791-1794) his bills for beer came to $98.67, a total of $1248.47 in today's dollars.

Apparently, however, his own beer was a hit. Surrounding neighbors asked for the recipe, and he even offered James Madison the opportunity to send someone during brewing time to view the operation in order to perfect it for himself. There isn't anything written to tell if Madison took him up on the offer or not.

Jefferson like most of the other Founding Fathers, also enjoyed the comfort and camaraderie of the pubs or taverns of the time. To colonists, taverns were not simply bars or places to rent a bed, they were more like community centers—the heart of the towns and villages.

June 11, 1776 found Thomas Jefferson sitting over a table in the Indian Queen Tavern of Philadelphia. Over the next three days, Jefferson drank Madiera wine and ale, and by June 13th he'd drafted the Declaration of Independence.

The Indian Queen Tavern, where Jefferson wrote the Declaration of Independence.

Taverns were lively places, and not unlike modern saloons in many ways. One way was in the drinks they served—a variety of concoctions popular in the day. One such drink the Founding Fathers loved was called the flip, a mixture of rum, beer and sugar prepared together and then speared with a red hot poker.

Taverns at this time were also important places for organizing what would become the American Revolution. Sam Fraunces Tavern in New York City, for example, hosted John Adams and George Washington before the war, and the Green Dragon Tavern in Boston—where the Boston Tea Party was planned—is where Paul Revere started his ride to warn Lexington.

On that ride, Revere was a bit concerned for his safety, actually riding quietly until about halfway into his ride. That's when Revere stopped at Isaac Hall's Medford Massachusetts home. Medford at the time had a very active rum distilling community, and Isaac Hall was one of the biggest distillers in the area.

According to reports, Revere had a few bracers of rum at Hall's home before continuing on his way. It was only after these bracers he began his famous, "The British are coming" yells.

The Green Dragon Tavern where the Boston Tea Party was planned.

Another Founding Father often present at the Green Dragon—as well as many other taverns of the time—was John Hancock. Hancock was a very active rum runner, smuggling the alcohol to avoid the Crown's taxes, and gained immense popularity in Massachusetts in 1768 when his sloop "Liberty" was seized for alleged smuggling. It was in these taverns he often railed against the King and rallied support for the Patriots' cause.

Original Flip Recipe (Without the Hot Poker)

This recipe dates from the early 1800s and would have been a drink the Founding Fathers would have had.

900ml of real-ale

100ml of Dark Rum

85g brown sugar (Demerara)

Grated Nutmeg (10 shavings)

1/4 tsp Ground Ginger

3 eggs (beaten)

In a larger, heavy based saucepan put onto a medium heat 300ml of the real ale. In a mixing bowl beat the eggs and sugar into a creamy paste – when the ale is simmering just under the boil, turn down the heat and whisk in the beaten eggs and sugar.

Whisk thoroughly and continuously as the eggs might scramble in the ale. When the ale has thickened and the beaten eggs and sugar have mixed and dissolved thoroughly add in the Rum and whisk. Grate in the nutmeg and add the ground ginger. Whisk thoroughly then add in the remaining 600ml of ale. Leave on a very gentle heat for 10 minutes until the Egg Flip is heated right through.

Turn off the heat and either pour the Egg Flip between two large saucepans or jugs to excite the drink, and make it frothy, or whisk it continuously for two minutes. When frothy pour the Egg Flip into heat proof mugs, glasses or tankards and drink while still warm.

Perhaps no other Founding Father brings to mind beverages more than Samuel Adams—now famously attached to the beer that shares his name. However, though most called him a brewer, Samuel Adams was actually a maltster and produced the malt for brewing beer, not the beer itself.

It was Sam Adams, though, who in 1774 wrote the non-consumption agreement. This resolution was meant to get people to stop buying British products and instead purchase items from the colonies. This included beer, of course, and Adams' hope was that it would encourage the drinking of colonial-made brew instead of English ale.

The war itself actually affected our future consumption dramatically though. In fact, historians attribute the rise of whiskey in America to the British blockade of molasses used for rum during the Revolutionary War. Prior to the war it would have been rare to find corn or rye whiskey in a tavern, but because that's all they had for eight years people developed a taste for it that they never got away from. There are blessings in everything perhaps.

Once the Revolutionary War was over, our thirst continued just as before. Maybe even more so. After completing the drafting of the Constitution, the founding fathers celebrated with 54 bottles of Madeira wine, 60 bottles of Claret (a wine from Bordeaux, France), and 8 bottles of whiskey.

And in 1783 Alexander Hamilton began practicing law in his native New York once again. One of his first cases was a lawsuit for damages to a brewery during the war.

Remember that these were important places that played important roles in our country. Even those places indirectly attached to the making or selling of alcohol were considered important. For example, in 1790 Congress was asked to approve an $8000 distribution to rebuild a Maryland bottle factory partly due to a shortage of quart beer bottles. The request was—unfortunately—turned down.

The Golden Age

(1800-1917)

This period marks a defining time for both the world and for alcohol. It's a period many consider to be the Industrial Revolution of the world. New countries were developing, wars were fought for life, land, and liberty, and scientific developments changed the way we traveled, ate, and even drank. Open any history book and you'll find out about all of these things and more.

But in this chapter, we won't be discussing the history learned from our school books or what we were taught in class. What we will discuss are the developments and discoveries made by man's drive and desire to distill a better whisky, make a better cocktail, or brew a better beer.

The Golden Age saw Lewis and Clark explore new lands, the War of 1812, the U.S. Civil War, Roosevelt riding with the Rough Riders and the Titanic's sinking. At the same time, though not as commonly found in the history books, Thomas Jefferson petitioned for a British brewmaster's citizenship on the basis of his brewing abilities, Abraham Lincoln opened 3 taverns in his home state of Illinois, Teddy Roosevelt was reprimanded for buying beer for his Rough Riders, Bass beer trademarked the first company logo (their red triangle), and Louis Pasteur developed pasteurization in the hopes of preserving beer longer to make French beer more well known in the brewing industry.

Beer, spirits, wine, brewing and distillation was a way of life. From wars, to political rallies, sporting events, scientific advancements, and riots, everything in our world was affected, improved, and sometimes even hurt by our love for alcohol. In this chapter we take you through what we consider the Golden Age of mankind's love affair with booze. This is the period we blossomed, the period when the magic happened. It was in these years that we learned, loved and perfected drink. Unfortunately following the Golden Age everything went to crap, but for a brief moment, all was golden!

The United States through the Civil War

The United States was an infant country at the turn of the century, and immigration was its life blood. Immigrants came looking for freedom, escape from religious persecution, reduced taxes, and the chance at a better life. With them they brought new traditions, new ideas, a drive to make their mark on their new homeland and a dedication to a better way of life for themselves and their families.

As the country grew, these immigrants settled the continent from East to West coast. It was "Manifest Destiny," and breweries and distilleries were setup in the new cities, towns, and states along the way. America was a melting pot, not just of ethnicities and religions, but also ideas, traditions, and innovations.

Some of those ideas led to the Civil War and freedom for slaves, while others led to new discoveries and innovations in beer, whiskey and wine-making. Some, more dark and sinister, led to the Temperance Movement and the strengthening of the subculture known as the teetotalers—people who refrained from or looked down upon alcohol consumption.

It was an exciting time filled with the growth of a great country, great ideas, and the creation of many of America's distillation and brewing traditions.

At the turn of the century states and cities, like the entire country, were finding and creating their own identities. In the early 1800s New Orleans, for example, was known for its barrelhouses—establishments notorious for their rowdiness and shrill piano playing. In the dark confines of these small buildings, customers would fill either their own mugs or mouths directly from casks for only a nickel. If people were caught passed out or no longer drinking, they were thrown out to make room for another patron who was eager to take his place.

New Orleans was perhaps the extreme study in the booze-culture that was taking over much of the U.S., especially in her bigger cities. Cheap rum and whiskey were creating an environment where to drink was to very quickly get drunk—often that seemed to be the point.

The term "Skid Row" dates back to Seattle during this time, and has come to mean what it pretty much what it was when the term was coined.

In Seattle, roads down hills were often paved with logs and used to skid fallen trees down. Because of the type of people involved in the logging trade using these roads—rough mountain-type men wanting drinking, women and gambling—it was common for them to become lined with seedy bars that catered to what these guys were looking for.

As an aside, a common and sometimes dangerous job was lubricating the road to make logs slide more easily. The person with that job was called the "grease monkey," which is probably the origin of today's usage of the word to refer to a mechanic.

Our appetite for booze at this time seemed almost unquenchable. But, more than one entrepreneur was willing to try! By 1810 the population of the United States had hit 7 million people. To serve them was 14,191 registered or licensed distilleries producing a combined 25.5 million gallons of whiskey per year. At the same time there were 140 commercial breweries in the U.S. producing over 185,000 gallons of beer annually.

It seemed like at every turn, wherever there were five or more people, there was a commercial distillery or brewery. Ohio had only become a state in 1803, but by 1810 it had one distillery in each of its counties making a combined total of 1.2 million gallons of whiskey annually. At the time it only had 230,760 people living in the entire state, and only 103,800 of those were over 16 (though that didn't mean a lot back then).

Not to be outdone, Kentucky in 1810 produced 2.2 million gallons of bourbon. And it had only been a state since 1792!

But the gold medal would have to go to Pennsylvania of all places. By 1810 the cradle of our country was producing 6.5 million gallons of rye whiskey a year. Its legacy as a whiskey-making state had been sealed by that time due to the whiskey rebellion. Now, however it barely registers as a distiller at all.

As can be imagined whiskey and beer were good businesses to be in. This was true for both the owners of the distilleries or breweries of course, but also for the workers, and in certain areas that was the biggest industry. This was true for New York, for example, when the fourth census of the United States (conducted in1820) reported that the state employed more men in the production of spirits than in any other state in the Union. Again, New York isn't somewhere we think of when we think of booze production, but at one time they led the field.

That word, "booze," by the way actually comes from this period. The term is based on the Dutch word, "bouse" or "bowse" meaning, "to drink a lot" and was recorded in use in the United States by 1821. Of course it didn't become popular until 1840 when a certain distiller named (aptly) C.G. Booze began bottling whiskey with his label on it. But it shows that people's mind was on the subject (drinking a lot, that is).

We also begin seeing in this period many of what we consider staples in United States (to drinkers anyway). The first true Western saloon was established in 1822 by a trapper named Brown in Brown's Hole, which straddles Wyoming, Utah and Colorado. The small hut was used by fur-traders and Native Americans to meet, trade and barter for goods, to gamble and (of course) to drink. Once abandoned Brown's Hole later became a hideout for Butch Cassidy's Wild Bunch.

Mountain men guzzling whiskey, 1800s

Not far behind the first true Western saloon was the first true beer garden in the United States. Castle Garden, which had previously been a fort and later would become an immigration station predating Ellis Island, opened in 1824 at New York City's Battery Park. Considering the huge number of Germans in New York this must have been a welcome addition.

The influx of immigrants into the young country also added to the rising number of distillers and brewers—naturally so because many of them longed for home and were happy to taste the familiar beverage they knew. In 1828 Irish immigrants founded the Boston Beer Company (the original one, completely different from the current brewer) because they wanted something other than English style ales or newly popular lagers made at the time.

Likewise David Gottlob Jüngling arrived from Germany in 1823 and opened the Eagle Brewery in Pottsville Pennsylvania in 1829. Naturally he was making a lager style beer native to his home and using natural caves to cool his product. Eventually the brewery would change its name and now D. G. Yuengling & Son is the oldest operating brewing company in the United States, and is tied with the newer Boston Beer Company as the largest American-owned brewery.

All of this alcohol-based industry fueled an American appetite that seemed to grow thirstier as the years went by. According to historians, by 1830, Americans over 15 years old drank over 7 gallons of alcohol per person. That is measuring only alcohol, not beer (with about 10% alcohol content per serving at the time) or wine (about 20%). That's like straight Everclear.

And that's about three times what today's consumption is. The consumption rate was about the equivalent of every American adult male drinking approximately eight, one-ounce shots of distilled spirits every day.

The increased consumption of hard-alcohol is linked to an early 1800s corn glut that dropped the price of whiskey enormously. Now it was about the cheapest thing anyone could drink. It also made whiskey consumption in the United States rise from about 5 gallons per year per capita in 1790, to 9.5 by 1830.

There was also a much different culture in that period. People simply drank all of the time. Up until 1830, for example, it was common for American workers to observe the "elevens," which was a break from work at 11:00 AM for a round of spirits.

It was also common for members of the working class to stop for a drink or two on their way to and from work. Booze was had with breakfast, lunch and dinner. You had a drink when you woke up in the morning and before you went to bed. Even President John Adams, considered a moderate drinker of the time, started his day with a gill (1/4 pint) of hard cider.

Crusading on a platform on the evils of drunkenness over the next 15 years, however, the U.S. Temperance Movement helped to lower the high consumption rate of the 1830s. Through politics, legislation and PR campaigns they drove the yearly per capita consumption of whiskey from an all-time high of 9.5 gallons per person, to one of its lowest: an average of just 1.8 gallons by 1845.

Even as the Temperance Movement gained steam and was helping to drive the consumption of alcoholic beverages down, breweries and distilleries continued to thrive, probably due to the huge influx of immigrants descending on the United States from Europe. The first brewery in California, opened by Willy McGlover in 1837, was opened under Mexican rule but quickly became popular.

In 1840, the Ballantine Brewery was founded in Newark, New Jersey. At its peak it was the 4th largest brewery in the U.S., and its beer, Ballentine Ale, is one of the oldest brands of beer in the country.

Not long after Ballentine opened we see the first large-scale commercial lager beer brewery in the United States established in Philadelphia in 1844. John Wagner brought lager yeast from his native Bavaria and ignited a revolution. By 1858, there were 30 breweries in Philadelphia, and the country quickly went crazy for lager-style beers. Other beers, like the English ales, soon fell out of popularity.

Lager beer advertisement from the 1800s.

At about this period in the history of the United States, our population explodes. We begin settling the West with a passion, and we begin taking our drink with us.

New York by 1845 had swollen with 2.6 million people, most of them immigrants. By that year the city had 221 distilleries that produced 17 million gallons of whiskey. Much was exported to other parts of the country, but if it had stayed that would equal just over 6.5 gallons for every man, woman, and child in New York.

In 1846 Texas joined the Union and in just four short years—by 1850—the census lists 19 brewers and distillers making mostly lager beer and whiskey. In 1855 Texas gets its first commercial brewery: W. A. Menger's Western Brewery in San Antonio. And by 1870 the Lone Star State boasts 27 commercial breweries. From nothing to 27 in 24 years is a spectacular feat.

Brewing was a profitable profession to be in. In Cleveland, Ohio in 1850, the few brewers in the city made $17,000 from 177,000 gallons of beer. That equals only $0.10 per gallon ($2.39 today) but a great sum at the time considering the low cost of materials and labor.

It was such a profitable industry in fact that breweries were going up about as fast as people could drink the beer flowing out of them.

In 1852 New Orleans gets its first commercial brewery. By 1890, 30 more of them open up. In 1856 Utah of all places gets *its* first commercial brewery as well. Unlike New Orleans there wasn't a flood of more to follow though. However it did have an interesting owner, Orrin Porter Rockwell, a personal bodyguard to Joseph Smith and Brigham Young, nicknamed Old Port and labeled "the Destroying Angel of Mormondom."

What's astounding at this time, though, is that in 1860, 85% of the production of beer still came from the breweries in just two states, New York and Pennsylvania. Combined, these two states pumped beer out of 1,261 breweries.

One of the largest in New York at the time was Matthew Vassar's brewery in Poughkeepsie. Its 50 employees were producing 30,000 barrels a year by 1860. In 1861 Vassar spent a considerable amount of his fortune and 200 acres of land he used to grow barley on to create the Seven Sisters College, now known simply as Vassar College. Vassar College, in other words, was founded through beer.

But it's no wonder that Vassar had the money to spend on the college, considering how much people in New York were drinking. Historians report that by 1860 (just before he founded Seven Sisters) in Albany, New York, inhabitants drank an average of 10 gallons of spirits per person per year! That's just in one city.

The people of Albany weren't alone. St. Louis that year had over 40 breweries. And that was only for its 160,000 residents. Actually there's little doubt they exported much of the lager to surrounding regions, but in any case 40 breweries to a city of only 160,000 is a staggering ratio.

Similarly by 1860 Brooklyn, New York alone had 50 breweries thanks to the influx of German immigrants arriving there in the late 1850s. Granted, most historians suggest these breweries were regional, but honestly the region wasn't that big.

While changes in brewing, production, distilling and other industries were occurring, an important change was about to affect where we drank as well. In 1832 Congress passed a law that would affect the landscape of Texas, all of the West and even the whole country. Congress passed the "Pioneer and Tavern Law" which allowed inns and saloons to serve alcoholic beverages without requiring the customer to lease a room for the night.

Prior to this law, booze was bought at taverns, pubs or inns. These were essentially the same type of business brought back from Europe when the country was new, and all of them had hotels or beds to rent above the serving areas. The new law freed the serving from the beds, and it paved the way for the kind of saloons and bars we are most familiar with today.

And this brings us back to the West, specifically to San Francisco. Fresh off its gold rush of 1849, San Francisco in 1851, with a population over 35,000, had 8 churches and 537 establishments selling alcohol. Now not all of these were saloons mind you, some were grocers and supply houses. But actually, in fact, most *were* saloons.

History does show that they were well stocked. One 1850s San Francisco saloon listed 110 different drinks, including Scotch ale, English porter, rum, port and gin. Just about anything

Toll Gate Saloon in Black Hawk, Colorado.

you wanted to drink that was made anywhere in the world could be bought. This wasn't even imagined half a century before. What's more, people's taste for alcohol was almost completely regional in 1820, so they wouldn't have even wanted anything that wasn't familiar to them. Times were changing.

Times were also proving that people loved these saloons. Leavenworth, Kansas for example was founded in 1854. But by 1863 it had a population of about 7,500 and 77 saloons.

Not too far away in Denver, founded to supply nearby silver mines, the city father's immediately saw to it that they had control over local drinking. Denver's first City Charter stated the city had the ability to license "tippling houses, dram shops, gambling houses, and other disorderly houses."

The backlash against drinking in the U.S. started in earnest during the mid 1850s as well. In 1851 Maine of all places enacted America's first prohibition-type law, which called for the suppression of "drinking houses and tippling shops."

Considering Maine's attitude it should be of no surprise that in Portland, Maine in 1854, Mayor S. Dow, nicknamed the "Napoleon of Temperance" sponsored and passed a law completely prohibiting the sale and manufacture of alcohol. This is the first explicit attack on booze yet, but only one of many to come. The Irish immigrants on the other hand saw the prohibition law as a thinly veiled attack on their culture.

After the law was passed, Dow authorized a shipment of $1,600 worth of "medicinal and mechanical alcohol," which was to be stored in the city's vaults. Ultimately this leads to a vocal battle over the shipment between Dow and a city alderman because the expenditure had not been authorized.

Dow's law had a mechanism whereby three voters could apply for a search warrant if they suspected someone was selling liquor illegally. After hearing of the liquor stored in the city's vaults, three voters appeared before a judge and a search warrant was issued.

On June 2, 1855, a crowd gathered outside the building containing the spirits awaiting the police's arrival and seizure of the illegal alcohol. The crowd grew in size to between 1000-3000 and a riot ensued. Dow called in the militia who fired on the protestors killing one and wounding at least seven. The event came to be known as the Portland Rum Riot and was a major contributing factor in the repeal of Dow's law.

In a twist of irony, Dow himself was later prosecuted for violation of his own law and improperly acquiring the alcohol.

While Portland, Maine was caught up in the Rum Riots, Chicago leadership was inciting riots of their own. Mayor Levi Boone renewed the enforcement of a local ordinance requiring taverns be closed on Sundays, and he also increased the cost of a liquor license from $50 per year to $300 per year.

The move was seen as targeting German immigrants and on April 21st protestors clashed with police near the Cook County Court House. The riots led to at least one death, six arrests and today are known as the Lager Beer Riot.

The U.S. had problems enough at home, and the world was changing. They were opening new parts of the globe, and dividing and then uniting the country.

Abroad, Commodore Matthew Perry sailed into Japan in 1854, forcing them to open their border. When he sailed, though, he brought 150 gallons of American whiskey as a gift for the Emperor. It's rumored the "gift" actually never made it to the Emperor, but apparently somebody enjoyed it: Japan soon signed a treaty agreeing to open two ports to trade with the United States.

And as bloody and gory as it was, alcohol had an impact even on the U.S. Civil War.

As the Civil War started, soldiers and sailors took their traditions and customs onto the battle field. A "lager-beer wagon" accompanied German-born Union troops during summer campaigns. Apparently it was a necessity.

Actually, for a time during the Civil War, alcohol wasn't taxed and the price was so low it was used for different purposes like lamps and bathing (the price of oil for lamps and soap had risen drastically).

The free ride ended on July 1st, 1862, however, when Abraham Lincoln placed a one dollar tax on each barrel of beer to help fund the Civil War. It doesn't seem like much but at the time, one dollar made a big difference. One dollar in 1862 equals about $21.00 today. Imagine the shock of people who'd never had to pay any taxes on beer before.

To make matters worse, Congress put a tax of $0.20 per proof gallon on spirits in 1862. In other words for every gallon of 100 proof spirits people were taxed. If there were two gallons of 50 proof each, the tax was twenty cents on the two gallons.

This hit home-distillers and sellers (the legal kind) particularly hard. Many distilleries closed during the Civil War not so much from the war itself, but from the taxes they had to pay on their product. Then in 1864 the tax was raised to 60 cents, which is more than the country had ever seen before.

Times were tough for any drinker at this time (as can be imagined), but particularly so for those whose cultures involved imbibing.

Take this story of a particular Southern soldier noted by a reporter who witnessed it at the time.

In 1862, during guard, an Irishman of the 2nd Tennessee Volunteers would routinely put the barrel of his rifle to his mouth, as if inspecting it. The odd part was the frequency with which he'd "check" his barrel. Finally, one day someone bothered to look and sure enough, he'd been filling the barrel of his rifle with whiskey. Records aren't certain as to what happened to him: whether he was courts marshaled, or maybe given the worst duty there was. In any case, he makes a befitting symbol for any war that Drunken History reports.

The United States beyond the Civil War

After the Civil War, America found itself in a very different place than at the turn of the century. There was immense tension between the North and the South, people who were previously slaves were trying to find a place for themselves among the rest of their countrymen, and the Temperance Movement was gaining strength.

During this period, the U.S. saw some of its worst disasters in history with the Great Chicago Fire in 1871 and the San Francisco Earthquake in 1906. As they demonstrated then, and do so even today, the American citizen is nothing if not resilient: they brushed themselves off, rebuilt, and made things better. Some of the biggest supporters of the rebuilding effort were local breweries and bars.

Breweries were expanding in size with Pabst and Schlitz leading the way for a new breed of large, nation-wide commercial breweries. Jack Daniels got his start, ironically from a pastor, and some of the first automated factory equipment was developed and used to make beer bottles.

It also changed alcohol into an expensive commodity. The price of Southern whiskey was dramatically raised at the end of the war, from $0.40 a gallon pre-war (about $5.50 today) to $3.75 a gallon afterwards (about $52.00 today).

Whiskey production became so lucrative after the Civil War in fact that by 1874 in Springfield, Tennessee alone, sales topped one million dollars per year.

At this time we also see the birth of the American Whiskey Barons.

As a young boy of 12 Jasper "Jack" Daniel's was befriended by Dan Call, a local Lutheran minister and storekeeper in Lynchburg, Tennessee, who took him under his wing and trained him to work in his store. It didn't take Jack long to become bored with dry goods so Dan began teaching him the art of making whiskey.

When the Civil War broke out in 1861 Jack was too young to serve, so he remained with his mentor in Lincoln County serving as an apprentice. He also transported whiskey to many of the Confederate Army's camps and forts, sometimes as far away as Alabama.

In 1863, Call's wife heard a fiery sermon on the evils of alcohol and so she and Call's congregation demanded he give up his distillery. He relented decided to sell his distillery to his ever loyal apprentice Jack.

By 1877, Daniels was producing 83 gallons of bourbon per day, making him second only to Tolley & Eaton, the powerhouse at the time that was cranking out 300 gallons per day.

Jack Daniels is now the biggest bourbon brand in America, still producing from Lynchburg, Tennessee, a dry county. The yeast currently used by the Jack Daniels distillery is actually descended from the yeast line originally used by Jack Daniels himself over150 years ago.

Distilling at the time was a huge industry in the South. In 1886, it was actually the biggest industry in Tennessee. Combined, the distillers there were using 42 million pounds of corn and 25 million pounds of apples and peaches per year.

In 1885 in Moore County, Tennessee alone (the home of Jack Daniels) you would find only 6000 people living on only 350 square miles. But you would also find 15 licensed distilleries.

Distilling didn't just occur in the South though, but across the country. By 1871, Chicago also had eight distilleries producing an average of 7.2 million gallons of whiskey per year. Unfortunately all were lost in the fire of 1871. Not all *whiskey* was lost, though. Chicago bar-owner and distiller Jim Gore rolled 80 barrels of his bourbon into Lake Michigan during the fire to save his supply.

Don't think the U.S. Federal Government didn't notice the huge demand for booze either. Taxes on alcohol at this time were driving much of the country. In 1885, for example, the Gibson Distilling Company alone paid $675,000 in federal taxes on whiskey. That amounts to about $21,132,879 in 2012 when adjusted for inflation.

In fact every year from 1890 to 1916, U.S. Federal taxes on beer, wine and spirits amounted to over 30% of all federal tax revenue.

With all of the money involved, it would only be a matter of time before the system became corrupt. In the 1870s a number of government agents, politicians, and whiskey distillers and distributers throughout St. Louis, Chicago, Milwaukee, Cincinnati, New Orleans, and Peoria organized with the purpose of evading taxes from the purchase and sale of alcohol. It's estimated the ring was able to siphon off millions of dollars in federal taxes through the use of an extensive network of bribes that included IRS agents, storekeepers, and rectifiers.

The organization was known as the "Whiskey Ring" and was finally broken in 1875 by U.S. Secretary of Treasury, Benjamin H. Bristow, acting without the knowledge of the President or Attorney General (who were both accused in the scandal). When it all came to light the episode resulted in hundreds of arrests, 110 convictions and over $3 million in taxes recovered (the reason for breaking it in the first place).

Moonshiners in the 1800s making tax-free whiskey.

The people involved in the Whiskey Ring weren't the only ones who didn't appreciate the government's take. In 1891, Alabama preacher Robert Sims—along with 100 devoted followers—disavowed U.S. allegiance and claimed the right to make as much tax-free whiskey as they wanted to. It didn't go over very well with authorities and over the ensuing months he was charged with moonshining and involved in a number of skirmishes with local sheriffs. Eventually he and his followers were rounded up by an angry mob and lynched.

Perhaps the biggest boom of the post-civil war economy, however, was happening in the brewing industry.

By now, the United States had seen millions of new citizens emigrate from various regions of Germany, and all of them brought their love for beer. In fact there were so many Germans involved in brewing that from its founding in 1862, and lasting until 1875, the United States Brewer's Association actually spoke German at its annual convention.

And their craft was apparently appreciated. The annual per capita consumption of beer in the United States between 1865—1910 rose from under 4 gallons to over 21 gallons per year.

You could blame the rise simply on the amount of beer being produced at the time. In 1865 alone, 2252 breweries made 3.7 million barrels of beer. Due to innovation in techniques the output increased substantially while the number of breweries actually dropped over the next 50 years. In 1915 only 1345—almost 1000 less—made 60 million gallons of beer per year. That's almost 15 times as much!

This period saw the rise of Beer Barons, like Schlitz, Pabst, Anheuser and later his partner, Busch.

All of these are studies in American success but none of them started that way. In fact most of them had very humble beginnings. Joseph Schlitz, for example was simply a tavern and brewery bookkeeper in Milwaukee before owning his own company. And even after taking over the brewery he worked in (renaming it in 1858) his business was rather small.

Schlitz truly began to succeed after the Great Chicago Fire of 1871. His company donated thousands of gallons of beer to the residents since most of the Chicago breweries had been lost in the fire, and they also built dozens of tied house (saloons required to buy its beer from a particular brewery) with a concrete relief of the company logo embedded in the brickwork.

By 1916, Chicago had over 7,000 saloons. Of those, breweries owned or franchised over 4,000, and Schlitz was one of the primary owners. This solidified the Chicago market for the company and launched them into years of success.

Another huge brewery today, Pabst, started as the Empire brewery in 1844. By 1863 the company, then Best Brewing, had grown into a huge regional brewer when Frederick Pabst, a steamship captain, bought a stake in it. In 1895 Pabst became the first U.S. brewery to reach one million gallons of beer produced in a year.

Frederick Miller founded his company in 1855 and realized modest success in Milwaukee and the surrounding area. Miller became huge, of course, with its release of Miller High Life.

Miller High Life, classified as a pilsner beer, was launched in 1903 and is Miller's oldest product. The slogan "The Champagne of Beers" refers to the beer's availability in miniature champagne bottles. It was one of the original high-end brews in the country (believe it or not).

In terms of success, though, nobody could match Anheuser-Busch. Interestingly they're most well known for the flagship product, Budweiser, but they were already brewing 16 different beers when they introduced it in 1876. Of course it quickly became their best seller.

It wasn't the only successful beer they made either. Anheuser-Busch introduced Michelob in 1896 as its premium beer, meant to appeal to tastes more accustomed to brandy or wine. It was the most expensive brand in the U.S. at the time, with a cost of about 25¢ per glass. That's over six dollars in today's money.

Woo-hoo! Best beer EVER!
(ad from 1907)

In 1906, Anheuser-Busch completed their St. Louis, Missouri brewery. It was the largest in the country at the time, spanning 128 acres. That same year they sold 137,722,150 bottles of Budweiser. The U.S. population in 1900 was only 76,212,168. That amounts to two bottles of beer for every man, woman, and child from a single brand of beer.

About the same time, in 1905, America's popular family-themed amusement park, Busch Gardens, was founded to promote Anheuser-Busch's beer. They featured rides and petting zoos, but they also gave away samples of their beer to make it more popular in urban markets.

The success of the Beer Barons of the late 1800s was due to a wealth of new innovative technologies. Pasteurization helped their beer last longer. The invention of refrigeration in 1848 allowed them to store their product, and ship and serve it cold. Anheuser-Busch created refrigerated box cars, allowing them to ship their beer long distances.

Even the first automated factory machine—the automatic bottle maker—patented in 1903, mass produced bottles, meaning that brewers could ship their product directly to the consumer instead of only by kegs to bars and saloons for distribution by the barkeeps. The bottle-making technology was complemented a few years earlier by the method to seal them. The mass bottling of beer wasn't made possible until the invention of the crown cap by William Painter in 1892.

Also astounding for the time was the sheer proliferation of small breweries. Though some like Schlitz, Pabst and Anheuser-Busch were getting big, brewing was still regional. Most people purchased from local breweries, so just about every place had to have them.

The great State of Texas had 27 commercial breweries in 1870 employing 77 people to make primarily lagers. Four of them used a new technology of the time, steam engines.

According to newspaper reports from the time, there were 41 breweries in Kansas in 1878. Oddly enough the IRS only reported 34 (think back to the whole tax revenue issue).

Los Angeles has been brewing since at least 1874 when the first known brewery of the area, the Philadelphia Brew House, opened and started brewing lagers.

Five years later, in 1879, the town of Tombstone, Arizona barely had over 300 residents, but it already had its own brewery—the Golden Eagle Brewery, which burned down and was later rebuilt as the Crystal Palace Saloon.

Earlier that decade, in 1873, the Golden Brewery opened in Golden, Colorado. Apparently, local miners liked the product. It brewed 3500 barrels in 1880, but by 1890 it was brewing 17,600 barrels. By then, however, it was known by the name we use today: Coors.

New Orleans had its first brewery in 1852, but within 38 years, by 1890, and with a population of about 220,000, it had just over 30 breweries.

By 1900, there were 60 Chicago breweries that collectively produced over 100 million gallons of beer per year.

One of the largest, Schoenhofen Brewery reached its maximum capacity of 1.2 million barrels per year by 1910. Imagine: that's just a single, regional brewery. Plus, it was in competition with national beers form Milwaukee and St. Louis. Yet demand was high enough for it to brew over a million gallons of beer.

The standard for sheer proliferation, however, was reached in 1879. New York City's 1.9 million people were kept happy by the beer of 124 local breweries—more than any other city.

By 1910, brewing became one of the largest industries in America, with over 59 million barrels of beer produced that year.

In fact, U.S. beer production increased so much between 1890-1910 that beer exports rose from 49,000 to almost

70,000 barrels per year. Finally, American beer was being shipped overseas.

The increase in brewery output, matched by the massive increase in beer consumption, was made possible by the huge increase in the number of saloons and bars that dominated the Western frontier. Every little town across the nation had to have not one, but many of these joints to serve thirsty locals. In 1879 in Leadville, Colorado, for example, a town built on silver mining, locals had 4 banks, 4 churches, 10 general stores and 31 restaurants. But, they also had 120 saloons and 19 beer halls. So while you could only find four places to worship, you could find 139 places to drink!

Likewise, Livingston, Montana in 1883 had 3000 residents but already had 33 saloons.

Santa Monica, California wasn't even a year old yet in 1875 when William Rapp opened its first tavern (the Los Angeles Beer Garden). It was also used as the Town Hall until 1889.

And Minot, North Dakota—founded in 1886—was only five weeks old by the time it had 12 saloons.

It's not an exaggeration to say that saloons were everywhere. Even while the number of breweries decreased, the rising output served a country building more places to drink.

From 1860-1875, for example, the number of breweries in St. Louis fell from 40 to 22. During the same time, however, the number of saloons increased from about 500 to 1200.

The poorer or more desperate a place, the more saloons would dominate the landscape. In 1900 Chicago's 17th Ward was the most congested in the entire city, with about 50 people living there per acre. However it also had the most saloons in the city at 118.

Similarly, a census of New York City taken in the 1870s counted 4065 bars below 14th Street (there were also three churches).

How many bars were there in the country? Experts estimate that in the early 1900s there was 1 saloon for every 315 people in the United States. 26 million American men over 18 went to 215,000 licensed bars and approximately 50,000 unlicensed (illegal) ones in 1900.

That same year in the city of Boston alone (which had about 200,000 adult men) approximately 227,000 people were patronizing bars on a daily basis.

The drinks at these places flowed like water.

In Dodge City, Kansas, for example, in 1878 there were less than 3000 people. However, they somehow managed to drink 300 barrels of whiskey per year. That's 5.5 gallons for every man, woman and child in town.

Many of these places served anything and everything you could think of. In 1880s Denver, bourbon sold for $2.50 a gallon, Mumm Champagne could be bought for $3.50 a quart, and gin was only .75 cents a bottle.

Because of the proliferation of these joints, bar owners would do anything and everything necessary to get people through the door. Many bars were actually bought on credit from breweries or distilleries. By 1900, 8 of 10 bar owners were tied to a specific brewery or distillery, making for bad selections because all they could sell was that company's product.

The bar owners invested everything they had into their place and had to be creative to get people through the door—low prices alone weren't enough. So bars began to feature fights or sporting events and gambling where it was allowed (and often where it wasn't).

One of the gimmicks employed was the practice of giving away lunch to patrons who were drinking. In fact this is the origin of the term, "free lunch."

These "free"

No free lunch! You have to buy booze too.

lunches usually consisted of salty crackers, dried pork, pickles, sardines and other salty food. After all, the thirstier people got, the more they would drink. In other words, you didn't really get a meal for free; you were buying booze at a higher profit margin. There's no free lunch after all!

While most of these places were honest, many were not. The term "Dive Bar" was first used in the U.S. in the 1880's to describe illegal drinking places or "places of ill repute" which were usually located in a basement.

Similarly, the term "Speakeasy" came from underground bar owner Kate Hester during this period. She'd often tell a rowdy crowd, "speak easy boys" so they wouldn't attract the police. The term became synonymous with prohibition period bars even though it was coined much earlier.

Even many of the legal bars were notorious for the wickedness that went on there. In 1890, Mushmouth Johnson opened the Emporium Saloon in Chicago. He kept it open continuously, 24 hours a day, 7 day a week until it finally shut down for good in 1906. For years without a break this bar was the center of depravation in the city of Chicago.

Then there was Michael "Micky" Finn. Finn was the manager and bartender at the Lone Star Saloon and Palm Garden Restaurant, also in Chicago in the early 1900s. In December of 1903 he was arrested on charges he used knockout drops to incapacitate and then rob his customers, leaving them in a dank alley behind the bar. "Slipping somebody a Micky" originated with this one crooked bartender.

You also didn't want to get drunk and pass out in the First and Last Chance Saloon in Oakland, California.

This was one of many places by the same name operating throughout the United States, but made famous specifically by two bars. The first was built in Kansas in 1869, and it was the *last* place travelers could legally buy alcohol before moving into Indian Territory. The second, and more notorious, was built in Oakland in 1883, and was the first and last place to enjoy a drink before stepping on or off a ship.

The rear of the saloon was actually on the bay of Oakland, and the rear door emptied out into the water. It was not uncommon to pass out in the bar, and then wake up on a seal-hunting boat in the middle of the ocean.

If this sounds familiar it's because it's the beginning narrative to the book, The Sea Wolf. In fact, the person on which the character, The Sea Wolf, is based was a frequent patron of the First and Last Chance Saloon. His name was Alex MacLean, the captain of a seal-hunting ship, and known for Shanghaiing drunks at the bar. His story was told by another young regular of the place, Jack London.

When Jack London was a boy of only ten years, the owner of the local saloon Johnny Heinhold saw him outside of his bar reading a book in the rain. The owner invited him in and that kind act jump-started the career of one of America's most celebrated authors. Many of his stories originated from the great deal of time he spent in the saloon listening to the tales of adventurers from all over the world.

Perhaps this contribution made up for many of the other acts that went on there (though probably not).

Another saloon of the West was made famous by Roy Bean Jr., a saloon-keeper and Justice of the Peace in Val Verde County, Texas. He called himself "The Law West of the Pecos" and held court in his saloon along the Rio Grande River. After his death, he became known as "the hanging judge" but records show he only sentenced two men to hang and one of them escaped.

Not everyone was so enamored with either saloons or alcohol, and it's during this period in America's history we see the dawn of the Temperance Movement.

Judge Roy Bean literally holding court at his saloon.

President Rutherford B. Hayes' wife, Lucy Webb Hayes was one of those who didn't approve of drinking at all, and was a staunch supporter of temperance. As such, booze wasn't served in the White House during the Hayes Administration, prompting the press to refer to her as "Lemonade Lucy."

Her view was shared by a number of the upper-crust, especially women. After all, from the late 1800s until 1919, "respectable" women didn't drink liquor (this all changed during prohibition, however). Though they did frequently use "medicinals" that were often up to 80 proof.

Another teetotaler, Dr. Thomas Welch, pasteurized grape juice to stop fermentation in the hopes of replacing wine at church services in 1869. Eventually his company, Welch's, would realize a fortune by selling its grape juice to families and children, but the Church (thankfully) still serves the good stuff.

To combat the rising number of bars in its state, Pennsylvania raised the fee for a bar license from $50 to $500 in 1888 (almost $12,000 today). The number of legal bars dropped as was hoped, but the number of illegal bars skyrocketed. This was actually the reason why Kate Hester (of the Speakeasy fame) opened her illegal bar—she couldn't afford the license fees.

The most severe act of temperance was exemplified by Kansas in 1881 when it passed state-wide prohibition. This shut down over 90 breweries across the state and put thousands of people out of work. At the time, brewing was the state's fourth largest industry.

Many saloon-keepers would find ways around these attempts at temperance though. In some places where the *sale* of alcohol (but not the consumption) was legal, saloons turned into "side-shows." Bar-keepers would charge patrons to come inside and view a "blind pig" or a "blind tiger." While viewing patrons were "given" two drinks with the price of admission. All perfectly legal of course.

The period before prohibition, America's Golden Age of drink, was a dynamic time across the country. There were new, lasting cocktails invented, like the "Boilermaker" (originally called the Shawn O'Farrel) in Butte, Montana for thirsty, Irish copper miners. And the introduction of new types of spirits, like liquor made from the distilled nectar of the agave plant and exported here from a region of Mexico (called Tequila) in 1873.

American wine was also beginning to flourish across the United States. Oregon, now known for its wine grapes, had grapes first introduced to it in 1847. By 1860 the state was producing 2600 gallons of wine per year. Though considering that in the San Francisco earthquake of 1906, 30 million gallons of wine were lost, Oregon's contribution at the time doesn't seem so grand.

This period gave us the term, "Hangover," first referenced in 1904 to describe something left over from the night before.

It gave us green beer for St. Patrick's Day in 1914 when a New York City social club dyed the beer green for their party. The news hit the local social columns of the newspaper and it's been in use ever since.

In 1910 the starting salary for a college graduate was $750 a year, a bottle of beer was $.05 and a whole barrel was $7.

Things were looking great for the new country. And then Prohibition happened.

The United Kingdom and Ireland

Though constantly in some type of conflict, England and Ireland found enough time to put aside their differences and get some serious brewing and innovation accomplished throughout the Golden Age.

The English drank from huge two handled mugs, invented the India Pale Ale, and created the world's first trademark. The Irish developed an Irish whiskey that today is more popular and cheaper than Jameson and, in the course of 50 years, increased the annual beer consumption by almost ten times. Innovative times for both countries.

Many of those innovations were in the brewing industry, but not all of them were in the form of new machinery or techniques. England's first trademark was the red triangle used for the Bass Brewery and registered in 1876.

Another innovation was a new type of beer. In the early 1800s English brewers were searching for a kind that wouldn't spoil on the long, hot journeys to Asia and India. Research and testing led them to discover that higher levels of alcohol and additional hops created an environment that was unfriendly to the bacteria responsible for spoiling beer. Around 1840 brewers devised the India Pale Ale. It was so successful during the 1800s it became one of England's most important exports during the period.

Another type of beer, Pale Ale, which was introduced as early as the mid-1600s became very popular as well, and grew phenomenally over the century. In 1830 only 50,000 barrels were brewed. But the English loved it so much that by 1880 over 3 million barrels were produced.

Porter was also still very popular. The output of porter in London breweries alone topped 1.8 million barrels of beer in 1823. Soda pop by contrast was just over a million at the time.

The 1800s also saw the growth and success of the most famous maker of stout-style beer, Guinness. Interestingly, most of its growth occurred in England, not Ireland. In 1840, three out of five of Guinness' beer sales were made in Britain, while the rest was divided between Dublin and the rest of Ireland.

Its popularity continued to climb so that by 1917, Guinness became the largest brewery in the world, with an employee base of approximately 3,650.

Its meteoric rise seemed to parallel the public's increasing consumption of beer. In 1851, the annual per capita consumption of beer in Ireland was 3.5 gallons per year. But by 1901 it was 26 gallons per year. No doubt, much of this was Guinness Stout.

At the onset of World War I, Guinness actively encouraged employees to join the British forces. They paid1/2 of the employee's wages to their families while they were deployed, and even guaranteed their jobs upon return. By the time the war was over, 800 had volunteered and 103 of those men paid the ultimate price.

Besides employees, Guinness lost its very first steam ship during the war as well. On October 12th, 1917, the S.S. W.M. Barkley, carrying barrels of Guinness Stout to ports in England, was torpedoed and sunk. Of the twelve on board, five perished and seven were rescued (all beer was lost).

London itself also had a tragedy involving beer, although an odd one. In 1814 a vat with over 100,000 gallons of ale exploded at the Meux and Company Brewery.

The explosion had a domino effect causing surrounding vats to explode and increasing the total amount of beer released to over 300,000 gallons. The ale poured into the surrounding streets like a tsunami.

The resulting flood killed nine people, destroyed two houses and one pub. The brewery was eventually taken to court and sued by the survivors and the families of those lost, but the event was ruled to be "an act of god." God really didn't like that ale apparently.

But the English did. Actually they liked just about any beer judging from the variety of those popular at the time.

And they definitely liked to drink it. In 1830, there were only 400 pubs in England, but by 1838 there were 46,000 of them.

The major increase was primarily due to England's Beer Act, which allowed householders to sell beer with a license.

The number declined eventually for a variety of reasons, including stricter legislation. According to tax records, there were only 8,425 licenses to brew and/or sell beer in England, Ireland and Scotland in 1883.

Unlike the United States, where the huge growth meant an exponential rise in places to buy booze, or in the production of alcohol, much of England's traditions and growth were static. Ultimately this meant fewer laws passed or regulations attempted.

Though there were a few worth noting. One was the reduction of the work week from 60 to 56 hours in 1875. The biggest part of the debate by businesses was not about allowing the shorter hours, but rather to decide whether workers should leave earlier or arrive later in the day.

Businesses wanted—and got—the work day shortened so that workers would leave early, because (they argued) if workers arrive later in the day it would give them more opportunity to drink before getting to work. Clearly, drinking and beer were still a big part of everyday life in England as well.

New laws would be enacted and put into place when World War I started, however. 1917, England's Prime Minister, Lloyd George put in place a number of regulations. He first reduced the alcohol volume in beer by 1/2, so that beer with the alcohol content of 10% was now suddenly 5%. The regulation was needed, he argued, because of the need for grains and barley as food supplies.

He also ordered pubs to reduce their hours by 2/3, meaning they would from then on close at around five or six in the evenings. Again this was done under the pretense of the war, but no rational explanation was given.

To add insult to injury, and again thanks to added World War I regulations, the price for one pint of beer in England doubled between 1914 and 1920. This came at the same time the alcohol proof got cut.

Perhaps due to these regulations or other factors beer production in the United Kingdom tanked with the number of brewing licenses plummeting from 16,798 in 1891 to only 1722 by 1927. If Lloyd George was a temperance supporter and trying to get alcohol curbed through means other than the obvious, he did a great job.

Meanwhile, another part of British life, though only around for a few hundred years by this time, was distilling, especially in Scotland and Ireland.

In 1815 England raised the taxes on Irish whiskey to six shillings a gallon. Instead of leading to a windfall of revenue, it actually led to the operation of over 2000 illicit stills.

There were still many legal ones, though. In 1781, innkeeper James Power established John's Lane Distillery. By the turn of the century his son had joined him and it was renamed John and Son Irish Whiskey. They produced 33,000 gallons in 1823 and by 1833 it grew to over 300,000 gallons a year.

Today Powers Gold Label is cheaper than Jameson and is the top selling whisky in Ireland.

1889 advertisement for Bushmill's Irish Whiskey.

And in 1887, the George Roe & Company distillery took up 17 acres in Dublin and produced two million gallons of Irish whiskey.

These were the best of times for Irish whiskey, but as with all things it was only temporary. In 1922, there were 400 distillers in Ireland, but by 1966 there were only 3 brands left due to high tariffs and low demand.

Likewise, Scotch whisky was gaining in popularity. The first single malt Glenfiddich Scotch dripped from its stills on Christmas day in 1887, making for a very Merry Christmas.

And in the early 1800s John Walker sold his own whisky, originally known as Walker's Kilmarnock Whisky, in his grocery store. It wasn't until his son talked him into distilling full-time that John, or Johnnie Walker, really began experimenting with the blended Scotch that made his name so famous.

Ultimately, the British loved booze as much as Americans did, and in the same variety too. When the Titanic set sail, for example, she carried 1,500 bottles of wine, 20,000 bottles of beer, and 850 bottles of distilled spirits in her bars. Just to ensure she had enough she also carried an extra 17cases of cognac, 70 cases of wine and 191 cases of liquor in her cargo hold.

From French wine to their own, very good beers, from whiskey made in their colonies to champagne, the English loved booze. And this was their Golden Age every bit as much as it was for America.

But to close off this chapter, since we're visiting the Titanic (poor choice of words, we know), we want to tell the tale of the ship's baker, Charles Joughin. It seems that when the ship hit the iceberg and was starting to sink, Charles did what nobody else in the kitchen did. He went to his room and drank. He drank for about a half an hour by his own accounts. Then he went up to the deck and began helping people into lifeboats.

After another half hour or so he went back to his room and drank some more. Finally he went back on deck and as the ship was sinking, made his way to the tallest point available. Unlike others who jumped into the water, he simply hung on. And just as the ship was about to go under, he simply stepped off into the water, not even getting his hair wet. He clung onto a chair and when rescued was perfectly fine. Many say he survived the icy water simply because of the amount of alcohol in his system. Lesson learned.

Europe, Asia and Australia

Like the rest of the world, Europe, Asia, and even Australia experienced a kind of "coming of age" during this period. Innovations, new beverages, and discoveries in the fermentation and distillation process brought about a prolific time for drinkers.

Among the many discoveries and innovations, Bavaria (Germany) and Australia both found that legislating or altering their citizens' alcoholic beverages leads to riots (a lesson the U.S. would learn later with the introduction of prohibition).

At the same time, new kinds of spirits were being introduced and gaining popularity, such as Dry Champagne and Absinthe, and Germany had by far more breweries per capita or by total number than any other country in the world.

One thing that was going out of style was a certain custom called, "groaning ale." Until the 1800s, people in Europe and even some places in the United States brewed special beer with higher alcohol content known as "groaning-ale." The brew was created when a woman was found to be pregnant, and then given to her during labor (an event that became a party).

Fathers and visitors would drink this beer and eat special groaning cake, groaning pie, groaning cheese, and/or groaning bread, depending on the local traditions—all of it made just for this occasion.

In some areas it was even customary to wash the newborn in the beer. We're really not sure why this went out of fashion; it sounds like a great tradition.

Something that was gaining in popularity, however, was Absinthe. In France in the 1840s Absinthe was given to soldiers sent to war in Algeria as a tonic against fever and disease. When the soldiers returned home, they brought not only a thirst for the spirit but word that it's an excellent preventer of dysentery.

Also in France, champagne-maker Perrier-Jouet decided not to sweeten a particular batch of champagne as had been customary up to that point. He exported the world's first dry—or brut—vintage to London in 1846. It was instantly popular with the upper-class who demanded more of it. The company still uses the same formula used 150 years ago.

In general champagne continued to gain popularity in England and elsewhere. In 1800 only 300,000 bottles of champagne were produced. But by 1850, however, production had increased to more than 20 million bottles per year.

Unfortunately for the French, though, just as champagne was gaining in popularity, the Phylloxera bug struck with a vengeance, changing the direction of the whole culture of drinking from then on.

The phylloxera enjoying some fine, French wine.

The Phylloxera is an aphid-like bug (actually a member of the aphid family) with a particular fondness for sucking the sap out of grapevines. They were unknown to Europe but native to America. Sometime during the mid-1800s some English botanists transported the clippings of grape vines from America to France.

The sad part about the story is that because they're native, American grapevines have a tolerance for the bug's toxic saliva, and can withstand the little buggers. European vines had no such tolerance. And so by 1880 almost 90% of the grapevines in France were destroyed.

The most popular drinks for the English high society at the time were wine, cognac and brandy—all French. With no supply they had to turn to other booze. And that's when their gaze went North, to Scotland. It was the Phylloxera that made Scotch such a popular drink. Had it not been for that little bug, Scotch would be more like Irish whisky, practically unknown.

Meanwhile in Belgium, the first Trappist brewery was built in that country in the village of Westmalle and began operation on December 10, 1836 (though the Trappist monastery itself was built in 1794).

Trappist orders were much different than their Benedictine cousins who'd dominated monastic brewing in the Middle Ages. Originating in La Trappe, France in the 1600s, Trappist orders were much stricter. However, like Benedictines they were charged with being self-sufficient. And so, like other monasteries, they brewed beer not only for themselves but also to sell.

Today some of the finest beers in the world are Trappist (though there are only six recognized Trappist breweries).

And as the production and popularity of beer increased in Belguim with the foundation of the Trappist brewery, records began to be kept about the type and quantity of beer sold. The first recorded sale of beer in Belgium was noted as a brown beer that was sold on June 1st, 1861.

Production and sales of Trappist beers continued to grow in Belgium, with some monasteries surpassing others in quality and the amount they produced. The Abbey of Scourmont at Chimay was the first monastery to sell beer on a large-scale in the 1860s. Chimay still sells the most beer of any other Trappist brewery, and is one of the most recognized brands from Belgium.

Not too far away in the town of Pilsen, Bohemia in 1838, the townspeople were dealing with a batch of spoiled beer. So, being the positive people they were they made a new recipe. They added more hops, mixed in lager yeast and a lighter roasted barley. Their new beer was beautiful and delicious and came to be called, Pilsner.

In nearby Bavaria, King Ludwig I was about to make a really bad mistake. In 1844 he declared a tax on beer, setting off the Bavarian Beer Riots that lasted from May 1 until May 5. Rioters beat up police and generally caused mayhem. Feeling sympathy for their plight, the Bavarian army refused to even get involved. Order was finally restored only after the King decreed a 10% *reduction* in the price of beer. He soon abdicated the throne to let his son rule instead.

Also in Bavaria and in the same century, beer gardens were created. Initially brewers would store their beer barrels underground near a river in a shady spot to keep them cool. These places were ideal to spend warm afternoons and evenings, so brewers simply put up some tables and offered customers the beer.

Throughout Germany in the 19th century beer production exploded. It rose from 556,555,000 gallons in 1880 (already a staggering number) to 1,139,500,000 in 1900. Only 20 years to double the output.

The German population also reveled in the burst of beer-related productivity. In 1880 the population of the German Confederation was about 40 million people, all enjoying the fruits of a whopping 11,564 breweries. Compare that to the population of the United States—50 million—and the meager-sounding 2,741 breweries.

All those breweries helped to increase the country's annual consumption of beer which was reported in 1893 to be

Gee mom! Thanks for the brewskie! 1913 German beer advertisement.

approximately 62 gallons per person, eclipsing Ireland's massive 26 gallons per person, per year.

And in the early 1900s production only increased. In 1905 the German kingdom of Wurttemberg, about the size of New Jersey, had over 5000 breweries making over 87 million gallons of beer.

Not to be out done, Hamburg, Germany (one city) had 5995 breweries making 100 million gallons of brew every year.

In total, the amount of beer brewed in 1905 Bavaria amounted to 450 imperial (22 oz) pints per "head of population."

By this time, the beer-drinking, beer-brewing culture of Bavaria and Germany was already profoundly impacting the United States. Virtually all of the large brewers in the U.S. were German-born or German-trained. However, many brewers began settling elsewhere during this time, specifically, "South of the border."

Almost all of the brewers in Mexico, too, were German or Austrian, and every Mexican beer made today was the product of one of those transplanted from that region. In fact, one of the most popular imports to America, a Mexican, German-style lager, was created in 1897 by German-born Mexican brewer Wilhelm Hasse. He began brewing a special lager to commemorate the upcoming new century. Naturally he named the beer Siglo XX, meaning 20th Century. We know it today as Dos Equis.

In other parts of the world, culture and nationalism were mingling with alcohol to create new and wonderful things, like in Finland, where the epic 1800s poem Kalevela originated from. It is widely considered the national epic of Finland and is credited with helping develop Finland's sense of nationality which led to independence from Russia. Ironically the poem spends more time on the production of beer than on the creation of man or the Earth.

Russia at this time was still producing fine vodkas, but was continuing to control its production and distribution. From the 16th to the 19th century people could only get and drink vodka in kabaks, government-owned taverns. Eventually people got pissed off enough at this structure that they revolted, ending the monopoly and gaining the ability to purchase vodka for consumption elsewhere.

But then bottled vodka wasn't introduced in Russia until 1885, prior to that it was only sold in 12.3 liter buckets. That's about 3 gallons of vodka at a time to haul home.

During this period we see the first brewery in Asia as well. Ed Dyer started a brewery in 1820 in the Himalayas to supply the English colonists in India with beer. The brewery, Dyer Breweries, made a much appreciated beer, called Lion, which was guzzled by the occupying Brits. The brewery, or at least its legacy, still exists in an Indian-owned conglomerate of breweries that had as their start Ed Dyer's facility.

And then, across Asia to Australia, the English learned a hard lesson in messing with the Aussie's supply of booze. In the early 1800s William Bligh (of the Mutiny on the Bounty fame) outlawed rum as barter in Australia. Riots ensued in 1908 in what came to be known as the Rum Rebellion, and it was the only successful armed takeover of the Australian government.

Lesson (hopefully) learned.

Leaders of the World

We often view our leaders of old as infallible. From Teddy Roosevelt to Prince Otto Von Bismark, our military heroes and political leaders are held in the highest esteem. But like any person who has ever been young and foolish or exploring new aspects of life, they too made a few questionable decisions and have left us with a few stories to tell.

The main difference between then and now is the lack of internet, TV, reporters, and social media that forever records and distributes evidence of poor decisions only to be discovered at the most inconvenient of times. Back then, it wasn't a lack of good reporting or of truth being withheld from the people, but a respect and understanding of youth and privacy.

After all, the bar tab from a political rally in 1806 that included 720 rum-grogs, 411 glasses of bitters, and 25 dozen cocktails, is a fact that you would never read in history books or see on PBS specials.

Something else you might not read about in a history textbook was an episode called, The Eggnog Riot. Over the nights of December 24-25 of 1826, The Eggnog Riot (sometimes known as the Grog Mutiny) occurred at the West Point military academy when cadets smuggled in whiskey with the intention of making eggnog (eggnog at the time was a drink of eggs, sugar and LOTS of rum or whiskey).

Eggnog they made, and drunk they did get. By the end of the night there had been fights, shots fired at West Point officers, property destroyed and general mayhem ensuing. The riot eventually involved over 1/3 of the cadets attending at the time, including future Confederate States President, Jefferson

Davis. It ultimately resulted in the courts martial of 20 cadets and one enlisted soldier.

While the Eggnog Riot is sure to surprise some, we must also remember the time period in which it occurred. After all, around the same time, Andrew Jackson advised in a letter to his friend John Coffee to bathe in whiskey in order to cure his arthritis. Drinking it probably would have done more good.

Later during this period across the ocean, Prince Otto Von Bismarck, who is often portrayed as the Iron Chancellor of Europe, was sowing his wild oats. Before leaving for college in 1832 his mom worried he'd learn the "detestable habit of drinking beer."

And in fact he did. He spent most of his twenties wandering from party to party (and not the political kind), until marrying his wife in 1847. She helped to set him on the straight and narrow and jumpstarted his military and political career.

The same year that Bismark left for college, 1932, Abraham Lincoln was becoming a booze merchant. After losing an election for state legislator that year, Lincoln and two business partners applied for and were granted a retail liquor license from the state of Illinois.

Although history books tell us he owned three "groceries" or "general stores" in the early to mid-1830s (a description thought to have been influenced by the Temperance Movement) all three establishments sold brandy, whiskey, wine, and rum as a primary source of income. It's also believed (by more than just us) that each establishment had a bar on the premises for the immediate consumption of the "groceries" they were selling.

Eight years later, in 1840, the President of Texas, Sam Houston married his 3rd wife, Margaret Lea, who was 26 years his junior. Margaret was able to convince him to stop drinking, a sizable feat as Houston had a reputation to be a huge imbiber. But he did. He gave it up completely. All he had were tall, daily glasses of "medicinal" bitters. Of course, bitters at the time commonly had an alcohol content of 45% or more.

But nobody before or since could match our 15th President of the United States, James Buchanan who served (or soaked) from 1857-1861. Buchanan was known to consume 2-3 bottles of cognac and a bottle of old rye whiskey *every single week*. To members of the press he was famous for his ability to resist the effects of alcohol in high doses. He would buy a 10 gallon cask of Jacob Baer whiskey every Sunday while serving in office.

Next let's consider the Vice-President Elect, Andrew Johnson in 1865. When he arrived at the U.S. Senate inauguration he downed three glasses of "medicinal" whiskey before entering to take his oath.

As he took the oath, drunkenly rambling with incoherent and slurred speech, he declared in a loud voice, "I kiss this Book in the face of my nation the United State."

Official records state he was "too drunk to perform his duties" and a senate clerk took over the process of swearing-in of the new senators. Imagine if anything like that happened today!

General Grant, meanwhile, *was* someone with a deserved reputation as a drinker. Abraham Lincoln once reportedly observed that he'd like to send whatever Grant was drinking to the rest of his generals (though there's no proof that he actually did say this).

However, much of Grant's legend was just that: legend. There is little evidence he actually drank as much as people think. However, there is one documented case written by a junior officer. Before the siege of Vicksburg in 1863, General Grant, called for a bottle of Old Crow he knew another junior officer had in his tent. Given the bottle he filled a large goblet and tossed it down in one drink. Now that's a General!

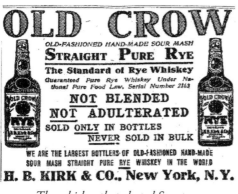

The whiskey that elected Senators.

Meanwhile, in 1870 future President of the United States Grover Cleveland was campaigning for district attorney of Erie County, New York. During the campaign, Cleveland and his rival agreed to drink only four glasses of beer per day to keep their minds clear during the election. It was certainly gentlemanly of them. However, they later decided it was too restrictive of an amount and adjusted the level accordingly.

One of the best stories of the time, though, has got to be from an 1885 U.S. Senate race in Kentucky. In the 1850s Old Crow was one of the most famous Bourbons of its time. But when the original distiller died in 1856, so did the original recipe. Luckily, there was a sizable stockpile of "original stock" Old Crow that was highly sought after and very valuable.

Enter U.S. Senate hopeful Joseph Blackburn. Blackburn knew how to win a Senate campaign in 1885 Kentucky. He offered people original stock Old Crow. And then he won.

Shifting again to future Presidents, 1898 finds young Teddy Roosevelt stationed in San Antonio, Texas, training the Rough Riders to go to war with Spain. Roosevelt was a man of the people, and so he often spent his time with his troops. Unfortunately he was spending his time with his troops at the bar in the Menger Hotel.

Colonel Leonard Wood reprimanded Lieutenant Colonel Teddy Roosevelt for buying his men beer at the Menger's bar. His reply?

"Sir, I consider myself the damndest ass within ten miles of this camp."

Roosevelt by the way is the only President to have been featured in a beer advertisement. And on his 1909 safari, President Teddy Roosevelt took over 500 gallons of Schlitz beer with him.

Yet, in 1912 Roosevelt sued a newspaper editor for libel after printing that Roosevelt was a drunk. Taking the stand, Teddy declared he had never had a drink in his entire life. By all accounts this seems to be ridiculous. However, in every illustration involving Roosevelt and alcohol it's never him drinking it. He's buying it for others or watching others drink.

The editor in fact couldn't find anyone to support his claims that the President was a drunk, nor anyone to dispute the President's claims that he'd never had a drop.

Roosevelt won the suit for 6¢ and an apology and retraction in the paper.

And so ends a look at our political (drunken) heroes after the Civil War. However, the next brief chapter is devoted singly to one of the greatest thinkers of our time who was also completely devoted to booze.

Then there was Thomas Jefferson

Everyone knows Thomas Jefferson was one of the Founding Fathers, the primary author of the Declaration of Independence and the third President of the United States. But there are quite a few things most people don't know about this gentleman from Virginia.

Thomas Jefferson was the only president to never veto a bill. He was thought to have been a terrible public speaker though his skill at writing and conversation were t thought to be excellent. He was a talented musician who loved to play the violin for hours every day (that is until 1786 when he broke his wrist trying to impress a woman). And, most importantly, he loved wine so much that it is thought to have been one of the reasons why he was always in debt.

It was his love of wine, dedication to learning, mastering the art of brewing and his desire to share these things with his fellow countrymen that sets Thomas Jefferson apart from other U.S. Presidents and their passion for booze.

From an early age Jefferson always had a fondness for Madeira wine, a type of wine from Portugal fortified with Brandy. But when he was sent to France as a delegate of the Continental Congress, it was like he was born again. He discovered for the first time in his life what wine really was, and he threw himself into tasting, comparing, guzzling, sipping and learning about every type he could find.

During his eight years in office as President of the United States, Jefferson amassed a wine bill of $10,835.90. This amounts to about $147,000 in today's numbers or $18,000 a year for every year in office.

Also while in office though, Jefferson was the party responsible for repealing the whiskey tax pushed through by Alexander Hamilton during Washington's administration. Jefferson actually was no fan of distilled spirits, and threw in with another signer of the Declaration of Independence, Dr. Benjamin Rush, who felt whiskey and rum could potentially lead to the ruin of man (well, that's exaggerating a bit but they really didn't like the stuff).

So why did he repeal a tax on it then? Because Jefferson *was* a man of morals, and he couldn't stand that the country would try to gain revenue from a product that many believed was detrimental to people. In other words, Jefferson did not believe in so called, "sin taxes" and viewed the whiskey tax as just that.

Interestingly enough, though, author Michael Krafft dedicated his book "American Distiller" to Thomas Jefferson in 1804 because of Jefferson's love of science. It was the first American book published on the topic of distillation and Jefferson even penned an endorsement of the book, stating that it was a wonderful application of science for the home. Indeed.

Jefferson's love of wine, on the other hand, is evident throughout the records for him in and out of office. It's even visible at his Monticello Estate where his wine cellar was 17 ½ feet long, 15 feet wide and 10 feet high. Few places in the whole country had a wine cellar of this size and few were able to hold the volume that his could. When he died he had almost 50 cases of fine wine in that cellar.

Jefferson also tried his hand at wine-making at Monticello, teaming with a viticulturist and physician from Florence, Italy named Philip Mazzei in 1773. The vineyard was adjacent to Jefferson's land, but was worked very little through the years since Mazzei was rarely there due to the Revolutionary War. In all, it doesn't seem like they were ever able to create their own wine at Monticello.

Despite not being able to grow their own grapes or produce their own vintage, Jefferson's house was always enjoying fine wines from Europe. Records show that Monticello would go through up to 400 bottles every year.

Jefferson also often gave credit to his daily intake of wine for his unusual longevity. 83 years is a long time for anyone to live, but exceptionally different at that time. Drinking wine (a lot of wine) on a daily basis is what—according to him—kept him healthy.

And as reported already, Jefferson was also a big fan of beer.

After leaving office and during the War of 1812, Jefferson petitioned for English master brewer Captain Joseph Miller to become a U.S. citizen because Jefferson wanted beer to be a common drink in America.

In his petition Jefferson wrote, "I have great esteem for [Capt. Miller] as an honest and useful man. He is about to settle in our country, and to establish a brewery in which art I think him as skillful a man as has ever come to America."

Miller was eventually granted citizenship and was later instrumental in actually establishing the brewing operations at Jefferson's Monticello Estate. In fact it was Miller who taught Jefferson's slave, Peter Hemmings (brother of Jefferson's favorite bunkmate, Sally) how to run the brewhouse.

Jefferson's favorite beers are reminiscent of his love for wine and other similar fermented beverages. Though no exact recipe for any of his beers exist, experts have been able to piece together one that is representative of what he would have brewed. According to many, it would have also been a very expensive beer to make at that time because included in the process was the addition of honey and lemon.

These ingredients obviously lent his beer a distinctive, complex and sweet flavor. But while honey was plentiful at the time, lemon was not—it had to be brought from the Caribbean and consumed quickly before it spoiled.

His beer would have cost three to four times as much to produce as one made by one of his contemporaries.

And so ends the legacy of one of America's most enlightened drinkers. While not fond of spirits, at least he was fair to them and didn't try to tax them out of existence. He introduced our country to the wines of Europe and spent years pursuing and perfecting brewing. Truly a learned man if there ever was one!

Adventurers, Explorers and Sports

The original celebrities of the Golden Age of alcohol were adventurers, explorers, and—somewhat later in the period—sports stars.

World exploration and settlement was still occurring as countries like the U.S. expanded rapidly. These journeys were long and dangerous, and with no form of reliable communication, home and loved ones were nothing more than a memory.

In order to make the journey more comfortable and to promote good health, explorers and adventurers would bring along beer and spirits to keep morale high and sometimes to share with people they came in contact with. These beverages also served as a source of reliable drinking fluids when water was not present or the quality questionable, much like the practice of sailors.

At the same time, the American sport of baseball was becoming a mainstream source of entertainment and news, as its popularity inspired the initial semipro and professional baseball clubs of the 1860s that evolved into the professional sports teams of today.

Brewers played a huge role in sponsorship and league development at the time and are owed thanks for their role in developing the World Series. The first modern day Olympics also occurred during this time period and it was rumored athletes partook in a drink or two before, after, and even during their events.

In 1804, at the beginning of our Golden Age, Meriwether Lewis and William Clark set out on their expedition to explore the Louisiana Purchase. A list of items taken on their journey included a .44 caliber air rifle capable of killing deer, silver medals containing a portrait of Jefferson meant to be peace medals, and various types of alcohol, including whiskey.

Each man on the expedition was given a ration of the drink, and it was a very valuable supply (running out meant there wouldn't be any more for a long, long time). During the journey records show that one Private Hall drank more than his share of whiskey near Kansas City. This infraction earned him 100 lashes. Needless to say he probably never did that again.

Barely 13 years after Lewis and Clark's journey, in 1817, another American legend, Davy Crockett moved to Lawrence County, Tennessee. He immediately set up three things upon arriving. The first was a gunpowder mill. The second was a grain mill. And the third was a distillery. Crockett thought the product of each was necessary and indispensable in the new frontier.

Later on in life, after being elected to the United States Congress, Davy Crockett made a motion that whiskey be provided for members of the House of Representatives and paid for with the tax revenue from the fuel fund. The motion, fortunately, never made it to a vote.

One of the most memorable events of the 19th century American frontier, though, was the Battle of Little Big Horn where General George Armstrong Custer met his ill-fated demise on June 25th, 1876. After the battle many reports surfaced suggesting that Custer's 2nd in command, Major Reno, was drunk throughout the battle. As most drunks do in that situation, he somehow survived.

Well after the battle, though, he was charged with drunkenness by the Army.

On August 2nd later that same year, Wild Bill Hickok was killed by Jack McCall in Deadwood, South Dakota's Saloon No. 10. He was holding what is today referred to as the "Dead Man's Hand," 2 Aces and 2 Eights. The reason for his murder is still a mystery though some believe McCall was either paid for the deed or upset he had lost all of his money to Wild Bill the previous day.

Many know about Hickok's death, but few know about the shootout he had because of the erect bull penis.

In 1871 while town Marshall of Abilene, Texas, Hickok was approached by several townspeople complaining about the advertisement on the side of the Bull's Head Tavern. It seemed that owners Ben Thompson and Phil Coe had painted a large bull with an erect penis on the side of the building.

Hickok demanded the painting be removed or covered but neither man would do it. So, the Marshall altered the paining himself, a move that infuriated Thompson and Coe. Coe vowed revenge, but within weeks Hickok ended the episode with two bullets in the once artistic Phil Coe.

On the other side of the country from Hickok's bull-penis episode, baseball was becoming the most popular sport for the young America. However, at the time it was a game of hard drinking brawlers. To clean up the sport, in 1880 the National League banned beer at all baseball games. One of the teams, the Cincinnati Red Stockings refused to conform and so were dropped from the league in 1881.

At the time, many teams were actually owned by the largest brewing companies in America. The ban on alcohol by the National League led the brewers in Milwaukee to form the American Association Baseball League so that their financially-backed teams could play (and crowds could once again buy their beer in the stands).

There was, at the time, a noted call to booze it up by many of the players. These weren't the disciplined athletes of today's baseball, but farm-workers and mechanics that could naturally field a ball or smack it with a stick.

Louisville's Pete Browning was one example of the hard-drinking baseball player of the time. He was so drunk during one baseball game in 1887 that after taking a 15-foot lead off from 2nd base, he fell asleep. Apparently, fans and players alike enjoyed a multitude of libations *during* the game.

Somehow telling was what Henry Chadwick, a sports writer of the time, had to say. According to him, 1/5 of all major league baseball players in early 1900s worked in saloons during the off-season. And most, he further wrote, went on to become bar owners once their baseball career had ended.

But to be honest, booze wasn't considered bad for your health at the time. On the contrary many found it improved their performance and so most athletes drank, even during the competition. One of the most famous illustrations of this took place during the very first Olympic Games in 1896.

During the marathon event it is rumored that runner Spyridon Louis made a stop at a local inn to drink a glass of wine. Later his grandson denied this saying his grandfather's girlfriend gave him half an orange and then shortly afterwards he received a glass of cognac from his future father-in-law (not sure if that is any better). Spyridon Louis went on to win the very first marathon, finishing in 2:58:50.

Alcohol of all kinds touched everybody's life in some way or another. Even if it wasn't booze itself, it was the scientific innovations created somehow for booze.

Scientific Innovations

Some of the greatest innovations ever created owe their development to man's quest to brew a better beer, distill a better spirit, and find better storing and transportation methods for these treasured commodities.

The Golden Age coincides with a time many consider to be a period of worldwide industrial revolution and with that revolution came new discoveries. Better crops were created that resulted in better yields of grapes, barley, and hops. Pasteurization was developed and its original intent was not for milk, the first refrigerators were developed and transportation of goods and people by air was beginning.

It can be said the Golden Age was not only a time of worldwide Industrial Revolution but also the time of brewing and distilling innovation.

Innovation began, as it typically does, in commercial enterprises, especially in determining the quality of booze people were buying and selling. Alcohol's proofing method dates back to the 1800s when payments to British sailors included rum.

To ensure the rum was not watered down, it was "proved" by dousing gunpowder in it and testing to see if it would ignite. If it ignited, sailors knew the alcohol content was at least 57.15% and the rum was labeled "100 degrees proof."

If it didn't ignite, it was considered "under proof" and of lesser quality, and then the sailors would most likely become upset. This method was used for years around the world and even on the American frontier.

To make better, more pure distillate (i.e., whiskey), better mechanisms for making it had to be created. In 1831, Scottish inventor Aeneas Coffey (who was ironically enough an excise officer who shut down illegal stills) designed the Patent Still.

The Patent—or Column—Still was invented to replace the Pot Still, used at the time throughout Ireland and Scotland (and in early America). Whereas the Pot Still simply boils the fermented mash, collecting and then cooling the vaporized alcohol steam, the Patent Still flushes impurities away and yields a higher quality spirit.

Though used throughout the United States for bourbon production, it isn't used (again, ironically) to produce Scotch because distillers argue it takes away too much of the character of the spirit.

Speaking of bourbon, the Sour Mash process for making U.S. bourbon was developed sometime in the 1830s by James C. Crow, who was a medical doctor from Scotland. Through scientific investigation he arrived at the conclusion that whiskey should be aged before sold. We couldn't agree more. The whiskey, Old Crow, by the way was named in honor of this innovator.

Another important innovation was gifted to the world in 1851 that's had far-reaching implications for brewing and the beer industry. In 1848 American physician John Gorrie invented a system to refrigerate water. He patented his system in 1851 and commercial development of refrigeration systems began in 1856 by a contemporary inventor named Alexander Twinning.

Refrigeration changed brewing because it allowed for mass, year-long production of lager beers, which must be kept cool to ferment. In fact some historians credit the desire to brew and ship lager as the cause for discovering refrigeration in the first place.

It also allowed greater distribution systems to be created through refrigerated box cars, built and used extensively by Anheuser-Busch. This in turn kept beer from spoiling and allowed it to be shipped greater distances. Finally, it allowed the consumer to drink a good, cold beverage instead of a tepid, urine-warm beer.

Refrigeration changed the beer industry because those who quickly took advantage of refrigeration systems in their production and supply/distribution chains—Schlitz, Pabst and Anheuser-Busch to be more specific—were the brewers who came to dominate the industry and survive through prohibition.

Brewers also benefited later in the century from the invention of mass-produced bottles as well as the creation of the crown cap to seal them. Both are still in use today exactly like they were in the 1890s. Before bottled beer you had to take a kettle to a saloon and have it filled by the barkeeps (who were benefitting themselves by the 1879 invention of the cash register by a saloon owner who wanted to keep his employees from pocketing his profits).

But bottled beer let brewers sell directly to the customer, and it allowed the beer to be sold and carried in something smaller than a metal kettle.

Distribution of beer was also changed in the early 20th century by the airplane. Falstaff beer was to be the first beer delivered by air in 1912. Unfortunately before arriving in New Orleans as planned the pilot drank the delivery.

Scientists would additionally play a great role in the beer industry. English physicist James Joule (who developed Joule's Law in 1850, still in use today by electrical engineers) began a scientific investigation to make his brewery more efficient by switching from steam to electricity. His eventual findings would influence not only the brewing industry but the world's approach to electricity and electrical engineering.

And according to historians, the concept of statistical significance—the theory that observations reflect a pattern and not just chance—was first explored at the Guinness Brewery between 1907 and 1935. That's when a young chemist by the name of William Sealy Gosset needed to find a way to experiment with hops, barley and malt without the expense of large scale experimentation.

His need led him to create small-scale experiments, but then he was forced to figure out how he could reproduce those theoretically on a large scale. His problem became a question of confidence. In other words, how confident was he in the results? The answer was in what came to be called the Student's t-test. Student was the pseudonym he published under (Guinness was paranoid about privacy and so Gosset wasn't allowed to publish under his own name).

This test is now used daily in economics and elsewhere to determine the exact same principles Gosset was trying to figure out. So, when next you're faced with understanding the statistical significance of something. Sit back, take a deep breath, and then have a beer. Preferably a Guinness.

But maybe the man who did the most for beer lovers was Louis Pasteur, the great French scientist. In 1857 Pasteur successfully argued in a paper that fermentation was caused by living yeasts and not by a chemical catalyst. This discovery led scientists to look for and discover new strains of yeasts that reacted differently and created new beer tastes and brands.

Later, in 1862, Louis Pasteur tried heating beer to kill off bacteria in the attempt to make French beer as successful as German beer (which never really worked as we all know). The process he used—heating the liquid just enough to kill off 99% of living organisms in it but not changing the taste—is what we call Pasteurization.

Thus the process of pasteurization was applied to beer 22 years before it was applied to milk (though the pasteurization process has been documented as a used practice in China since sometime in the 12th century).

The Creation of Cocktails

The Golden Age of alcohol is also fittingly the Golden Age of the Cocktail. Though their beginning can be linked to the creation of medicinal tonics or to Sir Francis Drakes' exploration in the 1400s (depending on the source) the cocktail quickly became a mainstay in society. The popularity and types of cocktails expanded quickly with many of them, like the Gin and Tonic, still enjoyed today.

Just like art, which had the Renaissance, the cocktail had its Golden Age.

The first recorded use of the word cocktail can be found in The Morning Post and Gazetter in London, England on March 20th, 1798. But the first use of the word in the U.S. was in The Farmer's Cabinet newspaper in April, 1803. It read, "Drank a glass of cocktail—excellent for the head;"

Then on May 13th, 1806 the first *definition* of the word cocktail appears in an edition of a Hudson Newspaper in response to a reader's question about what it was. The answer in The Balance and Columbian Repository describes it as,

"a stimulating liquor, composed of spirits of any kind, sugar, water, and bitters-it is vulgarly called bittered sling, and is supposed to be an excellent electioneering potion inasmuch as it renders the heart stout and bold, at the same time that it fuddles the head. It is said, also to be of great use to a democratic candidate: because a person, having swallowed a glass of it, is ready to swallow anything else."

Obviously, the editors of The Balance and Columbian Repository were not Democrats.

What's interesting about the description is that it is giving an almost perfect recipe for what we now call the Old Fashioned. According to accounts, the Old Fashioned wasn't called an Old Fashioned. Instead it was merely called a "cocktail" as it said in the newspaper of 1806. It came to get its name because later that century, people would ask barkeeps to mix them a drink in the "old fashioned" way, meaning with whiskey, sugar and bitters. After a period, it was simply called an Old Fashioned.

Recipe for a traditional Old Fashioned

2 oz bourbon whiskey

2 dashes bitters

1 splash water

1 tsp sugar

1 maraschino cherry

1 orange wedge

Mix sugar, water and angostura bitters in an old-fashioned glass. Drop in a cherry and an orange wedge. Muddle into a paste using a muddler or the back end of a spoon. Pour in bourbon, fill with ice cubes, and stir.

Angostura Bitters, the most famous variety of one of the essential ingredients in the Old Fashioned, were first created in the Venezuelan town of Angostura by the German doctor, Johan Siegertin in 1824. It was developed as a medicinal tonic used to treat the hiccups and upset stomachs. It took only 46 years for the concoction to be used in a mixed drink, the Pink Gin.

The Pink Gin was developed in Britain in the 1870s and is thought to have been created for members of the Royal Navy. This seems natural since Angostura Bitters were known to settle sea-sickness and upset stomachs.

Recipe for a Pink Gin

Angostura Bitters

2 oz. Gin

Splash a generous few drops of Angostura bitters into a rocks or martini glass and swirl it around until the inside is coated. Shake out the excess and then pour in the gin.

The British are also credited with one of the most popular mixed drinks ever introduced, one that is still immensely popular today.

In 1825, British officers serving in India were issued quinine as an anti-malarial medicine. By all reports, quinine tastes pretty lousy, so the officers did what any enterprising folks would do: they mixed it with booze to see what would happen.

The officers mixed the quinine with gin, sugar and soda water and the gin and tonic was born. Today tonic still contains the very same malaria drug, quinine, though in much smaller concentrations (if you put a bottle of tonic under a black-light the quinine will make it glow).

Recipe for a Gin and Tonic

2 oz gin

5 oz tonic water

1 lime wedge

Pour the gin and the tonic water into a highball glass almost filled with ice cubes. Stir well. Garnish with the lime wedge.

The first cocktail truly developed in the U.S. was created in New Orleans around 1850 by bar owner Aaron Byrd and was made with cognac, sugar and aromatic bitters. If it sounds familiar it's because Byrd created Louisiana's official cocktail, called a Sazerac.

Recipe for the Sazerac

Crushed Ice

1 Teaspoon Absinthe, Pernod, or Herbsaint liquer

Ice Cubes

1 teaspon sugar

1 ½ ounces rye whiskey

3 dashes bitters

1 lemon peel twist

Add the Herbsaint, Absinthe, or Pernod to a chilled rocks glass and swirl it to coat entire glass, discard excess. In shaker add ice cubes, sugar, rye whiskey and bitters, shake gently. Strain into glass. Twist lemon peel over drink, use it to rim the glass, place in drink.

Though known to every college kid in the world, Jell-O shots aren't a new thing either. The first recipe for Jell-O infused alcohol is found in Jerry Thomas' *How to Mix Drinks* (1862) under the name punch jelly. However, singer Tom Lehrer is credited with publicizing the idea when it was reported in the Book, The Remains of Tom Lehrer, that he snuck a Jell-O infused dessert onto a U.S. Air Force base that had banned alcohol for the Christmas party in 1955.

Original Recipe for Punch Jelly

Make a good bowl of punch, a la Ford, already described. To every pint of punch add an ounce and a half of isinglass, dissolved in a quarter of a pint of water (about half a tumbler full); pour this into the punch whilst quite hot, and then fill your moulds, taking care that they are not disturbed until the jelly is completely set.

Orange, lemon, or calf's-foot jelly, not used at dinner, can be converted into punch jelly for the evening, by following the above directions, only taking care to omit a portion of the acid prescribed in making the sherbet.

This preparation is a very agreeable refreshment on a cold night, but should be used in moderation; the strength of the punch is so artfully concealed by its admixture with the gelatin, that many persons, particularly of the softer sex, have been tempted to partake so plentifully of it as to render them somewhat unfit for waltzing or quadrilling after supper.

There were drinks of all kinds and flavors in this age. Many have fallen out of fashion, but there are some that still sound good enough to try. In an 1868 letter, written while in New York, Charles Dickens discusses drinking a "Rocky Mountain Sneezer" to his friend, M. Charles Fechter.

"If I could send you a "brandy cock-tail" by post I would. It is a highly meritorious dram, which I hope to present to you…"

Rocky Mountain Sneezer

2 oz. Brandy

2 oz. aged rum

Juice of one lemon

2 teaspoons sugar, to taste

2 dashes Angostura Bitters

Combine ingredients in a shaker and stir until sugar is dissolved. Add a handful of snow (amount will vary depending on moisture content) and shake well. Pour into rocks glass and top with fresh snow.

Jerry Thomas is the father of mixology. He wrote the first bartender's guide in 1876 and created a number of familiar drinks, like the Tom Collins, the Tom and Jerry, and dozens of others.

But none of his drinks were more popular than his Blue Blazer during the 19th century.

This drink actually created his reputation and he was famous for making them. In today's world we'd call him a flair bartender.

He would juggle bottles, toss them into the air and catch them behind his back. But the Blue Blazer was special because he would light the drink on fire, and then shuffle it from one tumbler to the next, all the while move his arms further and further apart. Until finally, there would seem to be a thick blue flame emanating from both his hands. Let's see someone in Vegas do that!

Recipe for the Blue Blazer

2 oz. Scotch

1.5 oz boiling water

Sugar for sweetening to taste

Pour the Scotch, water and sugar into a heat-resistant mug with a handle. Light mixture on fire. While ablaze, roll/pour mix into identical mug and back again multiple times. Pour the mix into another heat resistant cup with a lemon peel, cover to extinguish flames, serve.

By the end of the century, bartending and mixology was becoming both popular and professional. One of the earliest, but not the first, bartender guides was published in 1891 by William "Cocktail" Boothby and featured recipes for 20 cocktails.

That same year the premier pre-prohibition U.S. brewing school was founded in Chicago in 1891: the Wahl-Henius Institute of Fermentology which still teaches today.

Our Modern Dark Age

(1918-1934)

Prohibition, also known as the Noble Experiment, was the period in U.S. history in which the production, sale, and transportation of alcohol was against federal law. We have come to know it as the Modern Dark Age.

On the heels of the American Revolution, widespread drinking was on the rise. To counter this trend, a number of organized temperance movement societies were formed in the hopes of dissuading people from drinking. At first these societies pushed for moderation but eventually they pushed for the complete elimination of alcohol consumption.

There were temperance organizations in almost every state at the start of the 20th century and by 1916, over half of the states in the U.S. already had statutes that prohibited alcohol. A push for a complete prohibition would have seemed ludicrous only years before. After all, the Federal Government was getting 1/3 of its revenue from the taxes on booze. But then the passage of the 16th Amendment— income tax—suddenly made the idea viable.

Finally in 1919, the 18th Amendment, which prohibited the sale and manufacturing of alcohol, was signed into law.

While the 18th Amendment created a law that few followed, the Volstead Act (passed October 28th, 1919) gave the Amendment its teeth. The Act made any beverage containing over .5% alcohol—as well as the ownership of any item designed to manufacture alcohol—illegal.

America did not rejoice. The 18th Amendment and the Volstead Act were laws pushed for and created by the minority to enforce their morals on the rest of the country. It took a part of our culture, our identity, even our religious beliefs (remember Jesus turned water to wine, not grape juice or soda pop) and told us it was bad. The majority of Americans did what they do best when told to do something they didn't want to do: they ignored it, did their own thing, rebelled and found loopholes.

In short, prohibition was doomed to fail from the day it started.

Prohibition in the U.S. and the World

At the beginning of prohibition, several loopholes were exploited. For example, prohibition went into effect a full year before the 18th Amendment was ratified, giving consumers a year to stockpile what they could. The 18th Amendment didn't mention the actual consumption of liquor and as such, the Volstead Act was needed (and even the Volstead Act allowed alcohol consumption if it was prescribed by a doctor). Of course, according to rumors doctors became very busy at the onset of prohibition.

As the supply of loopholes and "good" doctors ran short, people turned to home brewing, distillation, and going to underground bars known as speakeasies.

Prohibition remains today a prime example of how not to handle the American people. It helped to establish organized crime, made millionaires out of criminals, criminals out of every day hard working men and women, and led to the deaths of hundreds if not thousands. In short, prohibition remains a prime example of an epic government failure.

Prior to prohibition's implementation those with money tried to figure out a way to survive until the whole thing passed by (many erroneously thought the Act would be repealed before too long). Millionaire W.R. Coe, for example, spent over $35,000 to stockpile booze from 1918-1919. That amounts to over $750,000 today. Probably not enough for a 14 year dry spell.

When prohibition did become law on January 16th, 1920 the nation had 177,790 saloons, 1,217 breweries, and 507 distilleries. In anticipation of the law's passage and implementation, most of these had made plans to do other things.

Breweries retooled to make different products. Coors, for example, had always made bottles for their beer but switched the machines over to making porcelain cooking items and scientific equipment during prohibition. Their brewing equipment was also kept running by producing malted milk and a "near beer" called, Mannah.

Other smaller breweries became even more creative; selling a type of malt syrup advertised for baking cookies but which could easily be used to make beer at home. And while few brewed beer pre-prohibition, home brewing (especially with the easily bought "baking" malt) became a smart and popular choice.

Distilleries also had to change. Some applied for medicinal licenses (medically necessary alcohol was legal). While others simply closed up. And the bars? For them there were only two options: they could close or move underground.

Amongst the bar owners in the country was Schlitz. At the time prohibition became law the brewery owned 57 bars in and around Chicago. All of them ended up folding.

But that didn't mean the whole city was dry. Even after prohibition began, Chicago still had 7,300 businesses licensed to sell liquor, and about 5,200 grocers licensed to do the same. Unfortunately, not all of them had stock. They were allowed to sell what was left, but no new booze was to be manufactured. So, fewer and fewer places had product as the years wore on.

Though the Volstead Act went into effect in 1920, many states got a jump on prohibition early, like Kentucky. When

Kentucky ratified the 18th Amendment in 1918—making it a dry state—Louisville alone lost almost 8,000 jobs virtually overnight due to the closure of alcohol-dealing establishments. After all, one of Kentucky's biggest and oldest industries was whiskey. For almost 120 years it had perfected the art of bourbon. Now it was all gone.

Enforcement of the law began almost immediately. In fact the court system became clogged with cases of people violating the Volstead Act. What's more it was tough to actually make the cases stick. Of the 7000 prohibition-related arrests between 1921 and 1923 in New York City alone there were only 27 actual convictions.

Ironically, though, any crime violating the Volstead Act—even carrying a beer—was a federal crime. And so across the country arrests and eventual convictions were made. The population of federal penitentiaries before prohibition was approximately 4,000, but during prohibition it climbed to 26,000 inmates.

Authorities pouring beer into the sewer during prohibition. Disturbing to look at.

Of course, the arrests themselves, and maybe even the number of convictions, were related to the mindset of the people within each place. It's estimated that in 1924, 95% of the population of Kansas obeyed the laws banning alcohol, but in New York City only 5% obeyed it. Kansas, though, had been dealing with a dry state since 1881, so maybe anyone that actually wanted to drink no longer lived there anyway.

On the other hand, some states had little interest in following the federal law but no way in overturning it. So in 1925, six states passed laws banning local police from investigating potential violations of the Volstead Act or the 18th Amendment.

Throughout the country, though, most people, businesses and organizations simply ignored the laws. In popular culture, alcohol was just as prevalent as it was before. Since 1921 for example, the fight song of New Mexico State University has included the line, "we'll buy a keg of booze and drink it to the Aggies 'til we wobble in our shoes!" Clearly some college students paid little attention to a law forbidding them from drinking (but consider that this university is about 30 miles from the Mexican border and it makes a bit more sense).

And in 1922 the Yankees made Babe Ruth sign a contract addendum that obligated him to refrain and abstain entirely from alcohol during the playing season. This was publicized in the papers and known about by every police officer and politician alike. Still nothing was done.

The law was simply brushed aside by most and forgotten altogether by others. While people couldn't drink publicly they simply found other ways to find their spirit of choice. The sales of sacramental wine to churches, for example, increased during prohibition by 800,000 gallons per year between 1922 and

1924. Obviously more people weren't going to church or converting. But more were certainly taking communion.

There was so much demand, in fact, that California grape growers—aided by (of all things) government subsidies—even increased their production of wine grapes by 700% (from 100,000 to 700,000 acres) in the first five years of prohibition.

And where there wasn't demand, inventive vineyards created it. Taking a page from the small brewers making the "baking" malt syrup, California wineries made a product called, "Vine-go," a grape-jelly that just happened to ferment with the addition of water.

If creative ways for getting drinks (like converting to Catholicism) were not available, there were a number of places that you go to quench your thirst, but most of them were underground.

Estimates suggest that in New York City alone there were between 30,000 and 100,000 speakeasies. This is in comparison to 16,000 saloons that existed *before* prohibition.

Likewise in Chicago by 1930 there were approximately 10,000 speakeasies in the city.

In Cleveland, an estimated 30,000 residents sold liquor illegally, either through speakeasies or simply at the back door.

But in states along the border, like Texas, speakeasies weren't even needed. El Paso, Texas—on the border with Juarez, Mexico—was suddenly one of the most popular "tourist spots" in the Southwest. And despite not being popular in Mexico, beer production somehow reached 50,000 liters per year in 1925. In fact the tax revenue gained from the sales of alcohol increased exponentially for both Mexico *and* Canada during U.S. prohibition.

And while prohibition greatly reduced the amount of Scotch exported to the U.S., exports rose meteorically to Mexico, Canada and the Bahamas. At the conclusion of the dry period, in fact, Canadian whiskey, gin and vodka were more popular in the United States than American bourbon and rye because our tastes had changed.

Crossing the border was actually one of the easiest ways to get alcohol. Aside from walking across the Northern or Southern borders, a booming airline industry arose to shuttle people quickly to the Bahamas or Cuba. And cruise lines were making a killing off of the "Booze Cruise," essentially a cruise out to international waters where passengers could drink as much as they wanted.

For those without the means of convenient transport, though, it was the speakeasies that filled the bill.

The illegal bars that were set up around the country could range in quality, class and style. Some had velvet, polished wood and brass rails. Others though were little more than a small, smoky room and a card table.

Some were considered every bit as much high society as the fashionable spots the upper-crust went to before the Volstead Act, while others were dangerous dives that you didn't want to be caught in past dark.

The speakeasies are credited with opening the nightlife and even drinking to women. Before prohibition most bars and saloons only allowed men and maybe had a small room off to the side for a lady to sip her medicinal. The only women frequenting bars at that time were the kind that got paid to do so.

But in prohibition, ironically enough, women were liberated. It was already illegal, after all, so why not?

Many of the mixed cocktails we know and love today were founded in the speakeasies, mainly as a method to hide the taste of the low-quality booze they were selling.

The martini, for example, became a popular drink during the 1920s because of the availability of gin, and even the martini glass was invented in the speakeasy. The glass could keep drinks cold by allowing people to hold it by the stem, and one could quickly finish the drink in case of a raid because of its wide mouth.

The stuff served at these places was often simple rotgut. The term "Bathtub Gin" became a popular term for describing most of it, though only some of it was gin and none of it was actually made in the bathtub.

Moonshiners would add water to the bottles of booze they supplied and the bottle they preferred was too tall to be filled in the sink and so was filled in the bathtub.

Often this stuff was dangerous and made by people who didn't know what they were doing or simply didn't care because they were trying to make money. Historians estimate that up to 50,000 people were blinded or paralyzed from bad liquor during prohibition.

But this simply didn't stop people from getting it, especially the hard stuff.

Though it was created to get the U.S. off the bottle (especially distilled spirits), experts believe that alcohol consumption increased by 11.6% total during prohibition. Beer consumption did fall between 1919 and 1933 but the consumption of hard liquor actually increased by 15% during prohibition (and ironically dropped 25% *after* repeal).

This brings up the one thing prohibition did provide: crime. Almost immediately after the Volstead Act was passed and enforcement went into effect, nickel and dime hoods became bootleggers and speakeasy owners. Within time, the war between the various organizations and characters became a bloody war on the streets of American cities, culminating in the Saint Valentine's Day Massacre in 1929.

These bootleggers spread from coast to coast and created networks of liquor manufacturing and distribution. The most famous and notorious were the names out of New York (like Dutch Schultz) and Chicago (like Al Capone). But even out West entrepreneurs were lining up to keep people soaked.

Like Albert Marco, who was credited with introducing Los Angeles to Canadian whiskey and earning over $500,000 between 1922 and 1924 from bootlegging.

Speaking of Los Angeles, Hollywood, initially on board and celebrating prohibition (now that people weren't going to bars they could go to the movies), became disillusioned by the end of the decade. A study of films released between 1929 and 1931 found 43% of them showed intoxication and 66% showed drinking alcoholic beverages.

Support started to erode even more after the economic collapse of the stock market in 1929.

In 1930, the New York Times estimated that the U.S. Government was losing $500 million per year in taxes due to the enactment and enforcement of the Volstead Act.

Similarly in January 1932, U.S. Senator Tydings (Maryland) argued that re-legalizing beer would create 300,000 jobs in 24 hours.

Snatching upon this sentiment, Franklin D. Roosevelt promised to repeal prohibition if elected president. The populism of his message took hold and, as we know, he was elected in 1932. He was sworn into office on March 4th, 1933 and 19 days later signed the Cullen-Harrison Act on March 23rd allowing for the manufacture and sale of 3.2% beer—a start to be sure, but a sign that he would stick to his word and try to help the American people.

When prohibition ended, Pearl Brewing Company flew their beer all over the nation (courtesy Pearl Brewing Company).

Upon signing the Act, FDR is famously quoted as declaring, "I believe this would be a good time for a beer." Within minutes, a delivery truck from the Washington D.C.-based Abner-Drury Brewery delivered 2 cases to him amidst much fanfare. The beer was passed out to the press, making the President instantly loved by the reporters.

Prohibition finally ended on December 5th, 1933 with the ratification of the 21st Amendment. Temperance supporters had to admit that, though the experiment was noble, it had certainly failed.

Coincidentally, on the night of December 5th 1933, there just happened to be 50,000 gallons of imported liquor on hand in New Orleans. The same was true all over the country, and the celebrations lasted for days in some cases.

That year—in 1933—the United States imported only 7000 barrels of beer. But by 1937 they drastically increased the number of imported barrels to 68,000.

And, also in 1933, the top sources of federal taxes were income tax, cigarette tax…and taxes on alcohol. Nothing really changed.

When prohibition was finally repealed, the Great Depression had taken root. Many hoped and believed that brewers and distillers would go right back to work, thousands of jobs would be created, and the country would go back to the way it was during pre-prohibition. But it didn't.

And as the country woke up from the nightmare that was prohibition, the hangover known as the Great Depression was in full swing.

To make matters worse, we had to rebuild a brewing and distilling industry in the midst of economic turmoil. Much of the pre-prohibition distilled whiskey was prescribed by doctors under special licenses until 1934, so there wasn't much left.

Before prohibition, St. Louis had 22 breweries, but only nine reopened in 1933. In all there were approximately 1200 breweries in the U.S. in 1918, but only 750 by the start of 1934.

And *five years* after the repeal, 10% of U.S. breweries closed because they couldn't compete with Anheuser-Busch, Pabst, and Schlitz.

In fact, prohibition turned out to be the best thing that happened to the Beer Barons, because it ended up closing all of their smaller, regional competition.

Perhaps to cap it all off, at the end of the Noble Experiment we had a new sport. The National Association of Stock Car Racing—NASCAR—got its start because Southerners were tricking out their cars to run booze during prohibition in an attempt to flee law enforcement.

The Modern Age

(1934-Present)

As Prohibition ended, the Modern Age of alcohol began.

The Great Depression was in full swing when the 21st Amendment was ratified, and some argue it wouldn't have been as *Great* without the assistance of prohibition.

The 18th Amendment not only caused hundreds of businesses to close and thousands to lose their jobs, but it shorted the government millions and possibly billions of dollars in tax revenue during one of the most successful times of the country (the 1920s). It also put huge strains on the welfare and penal system as brewery and distillery employees flooded the unemployment system.

But fortunately there was a light at the end of the tunnel, unfortunately it was a war. Many historians agree that the increase in government spending leading up to America's entry into WWII was the beginning of the end of the Great Depression.

When America finally entered the war in 1941 the last effects of the Great Depression were shrugged off and the industry of the U.S., described by the Japanese Admiral Yamamoto as a "sleeping giant," awoke.

Prohibition had greatly changed the country when the Modern Age began. Add in the Great Depression, World War II, the Civil Rights Movements, and the period in which the cocktail grew from infancy into its prime and you have one of the greatest periods in alcohol's extensive history.

The Modern Era through World War II

The Modern Era Begins with the end of Prohibition and the beginning of the Great Depression. Many breweries and distilleries reopened hoping to find a new frenzied demand for their products. Instead they found a country where most couldn't afford to pay for the luxury of a drink. The breweries and distilleries that had made it through prohibition were again looking at closing down due to the lack of customers.

As the world geared up for World War II the U.S. began to exit the Great Depression and breweries and distilleries were again solvent. As citizens from around the world mingled so did our love for libations. Irish whiskey became popular in the U.S., breweries set aside portions of their products just for the military, and the leaders who drank were the ones who conquered.

The period started, though, with a fairly simple innovation: the beer can.

The Gottfried Krueger Brewing Company, which produced Krueger Beer, was the first to produce beer in cans, beginning on January 24, 1935.

This wasn't the beginning of the story though. The American Can Company had been trying to create a beer can since 1909, but found it was actually pretty difficult to do. First, the cans had to be lined, otherwise the beer would react to the metals themselves—rusting them or spoiling the beer. Second, the cans had to withstand the pressure of the carbonated beverage inside it (which was up to 80 pounds per square inch).

Prohibition—naturally—put a stop to their endeavors but they started to again look for a solution in 1933. By 1935 they'd solved their problems, lining the can with a type of plastic and making it strong enough to hold the beer yet light enough to be practical and cheaper than glass.

While Pabst and Anheuser-Busch were both interested they were afraid of committing until they saw how people reacted to it in the marketplace. Enter Gottfried Krueger Brewing Company, which was small enough to really not have that much to lose.

The Krueger Brewing Company cans were so popular that by the end of the year, 37 breweries were selling their beer in cans too.

Ironically though, it was Pabst who, in the early1940s, would become the first brewer to sell 6-packs of beer (in cans). Pabst decided on a 6-pack instead of another number because they said it was the ideal size for "wives to fit it in the shopping basket."

Seeing the success of the American brewers, the English decided to can their beer also. The first company to can beer outside of the U.S. was the Felinfoel Brewery of Wales, which canned their Pale Ale for the first time in December of 1935.

While many beer companies were turning to steel cans, one brewer—Rolling Rock—was developing the famous '33' bottles.

There are numerous speculations as to why the '33' is printed on their bottles. Some say it is because prohibition ended in 1933. Others insist it refers to the year the Pittsburgh Steelers were formed (their team practices are held in Latrobe).

Yet, some think it refers to the number of words in the slogan, or that it was simply a printing error. Truth be told, no one knows the true origin of the '33' and it remains one of the great mysteries in the world of beer.

A year after cans were developed, in 1936, another seemingly simple innovation changed the delivery of beer. The Red Barrel pasteurized beer with artificial carbonation was introduced in England, allowing beer to be dispensed from pressurized kegs instead of through pump-type setups. But the technique wasn't immediately popular or even used until the 1960s. Without the system though, all those trendy craft beer bars springing up around American wouldn't exist.

At the end of the decade, the very first female U.S. brewery CEO Emma Koehler, resigned her positioned. She successfully took over and ran San Antonio's Pearl Brewery after her husband died in 1914. She steered the company through prohibition, keeping its assets and seeing it revived in 1933 before finally resigning in 1940.

Similarly, the end of the decade saw the only woman to ever head a *major* brewing company take her position as head of Miller Brewing. Elise Miller John inherited the company from her father, Frederick Miller in 1938 and ran the operation until 1946.

Aside from the brewing industry, there were a fair number of cocktails invented during this short period.

The Hurricane was developed by New Orleans bar owner Pat O'Brien in the early 1940s. He created it to help him get rid of all of the less popular rum that local distributors forced him to buy before he could purchase any of the more popular liquors like whiskey and Scotch.

Another rum-based drink, the Mai Tai, from the Tahitian word for "good," was NOT invented in Hawaii, but in Oakland, California by Victor Bergeron at the one and only Trader Vic's in 1944.

Trader Vic's rival, Don the Beachcomber (outside of Los Angeles) claimed to have created the Mai Tai in 1933, but the claim was made well after Trader Vic's introduction of the drink. And while the drink is similar, it is also vastly different in ingredients and taste.

We also get the first reference to a word used at bars every single minute of every day: shot. The first use of the word "shot" in the media in reference to an alcohol measurement was in a 1940s New York Times article. The word had been around for a time already, but nobody is really sure exactly where it originated from.

The tequila industry was growing as well, and exporting much more spirit to the United States, which undoubtedly discovered the liquor during jaunts to Mexico during prohibition. About this time certain distillers, usually from the state of Oaxaca, Mexico, placed a worm or moth larvae into the bottle during bottling. Though it is thought to affect the flavor, the practice began as a marketing ploy.

There was also the innovation in 1938 that ruined the drunken joy-ride after too many of those cocktails and shots of tequila: the drunk-o-meter—the first breath-testing instrument created to measure a person's alcohol levels.

To use the drunk-o-meter a person would first blow into a balloon. The air in the balloon—their breath—was released into a chemical solution and if there was alcohol present, the solution changed color. The more alcohol that was present, the greater the color change. The level of alcohol in a person's blood could then be estimated by a simple equation.

And then of course, this period saw the triumph of good over evil during World War II.

What's interesting in this episode of world history is that it pits two men against each other with views about drinking that were as different as could be. Winston Churchill was notorious for the amount of alcohol he regularly consumed. His preferences included pretty much everything, and he was fastidious about his drinks.

He would often order a dry martini and then demand that the bartender place the bottle of vermouth on the bar so he was sure it wasn't added. He was frequently called a drunk, a sot and worse.

And then there was Adolf Hitler. Hitler was, to put it mildly, a teetotaler. He did not drink and actually looked down with scorn on those who did. He thought it weakened you and then of course it was all just a big Jewish conspiracy to control the master race.

In the end, we all know who won: the drunk.

The German people were not very much like their leader. They were still a beer-crazy people no matter what the little nut-job with the moustache told them (paranoia and brain-washing only go so far).

But the war did put a crimp in their supply. From 1938 until 1945, the production of beer in Germany—once the champion of the world—dropped by 20 million gallons.

In contrast, production in the United Kingdom actually rose by eight million gallons. Similarly from when the U.S. entered WWII in 1941 until the end in 1945, the overall production of beer increased by over 40% even though the number of breweries decreased.

15% of beer during WWII went to the troops.

These increases in production at a time when ingredients and resources were scarcer than ever was partly due to new innovative techniques in brewing, but maybe also due to a sense of patriotism. At the time the U.S. government required breweries to allocate 15% of their beer production for the military to boost the morale of the troops.

Likewise, British breweries were sending their product across the channel to help their own boys. Perhaps the most famous episode illustrating this was the use of their fighter planes—the Spitfire's—to carry beer to Normandy.

To help the British troops the Heneger and Constable Brewery donated free beer to the military. It was certainly appreciated, but the logistics of equipping the troops with vital supplies was already a challenge causing little chance to get non-necessary supplies successfully to the troops.

However, shortly after the D-Day Invasion, it was discovered that a Spitfire's pylons, normally used for carrying bombs or fuel tanks, could be modified to carry beer kegs. As such, the stream of free beer began to flow to British troops in Normandy.

Pilots of the Spitfire's would often fly at high altitudes in order to cool and refresh the beer. This often led to them arriving with chilled and ready-to-drink beer upon landing.

Later, they began to use long range fuel tanks modified to carry beer instead of fuel. The modification even received the official designation of Mod XXX.

Unfortunately the operation was cut short when the brewery was notified it would be fined for not paying excise taxes on the beer it was exporting out of the country. Truly an asinine moment in human history if ever there was one.

America meanwhile was learning it's hard to take alcohol away from a country that just won back its right to drink it. Americans at the time were finding a taste for the imported tequila (worm and all) because European spirits were no longer available. In fact tequila demand in the U.S rose by 110% between 1940 and 1950.

Even in the most miserable of places, the prisoner of war camps, the ingenuity of the boozer would go undaunted. Prisoners at the Colditz Prisoners of War Camp, specifically, stayed busy by making moonshine from yeast, water, German jam and Red Cross sugar.

And while occupying Japan, many U.S. soldiers grew thirsty for American bourbon. Japanese merchants were only too happy to oblige. From this brief episode we get the now notorious story of these same merchants selling fake bourbon with the label that read, "Famous in Philadelphia Since 1486."

When the American soldier came back from the war they brought a thirst for another spirit with them. Irish whiskey, rarely consumed in the United States suddenly became popular.

At the end of the war things were finally getting back to normal. Breweries in the states were picking up production again, and America was entering a boom economy. Beer and spirit sales soared. Because of the interruption of World War II imported beer in the U.S. had fallen from 68,000 barrels in 1937, to only 34,000 barrels in 1940.

But it skyrocketed again by 1946 to over 385,000 for a thirsty nation about to face the Cold War, the Space Race, and the hippies.

The End of the War through Today

As the world exited from the strife and chaos of World War II innovations in the world of alcohol continued at break neck speeds. New records were set, and women were finally allowed into all drinking establishments (with a little help from the Supreme Court), and taxes were raised (yet again).

Americans were a changed people, with new ideas, a new outlook on life and even a new lexicon. For example, the first written use of the term, "Shit-Faced" was from a 1948 linguistic study of World War II vets at the University of Texas at Arlington. Apparently they used the acronym, S.F.C. which stood for Shit-Faced Charley, meaning "an undesirable person."

But with all of the innovations, all of the records set, and all we'd learned over the last 10,000 plus years of drinking, we had yet to find that perfect little pill that cured and or prevented the forever present hangover. Strange. We could put a man on the moon (and return him safely to Earth), but we still got headaches when we drank one beer too many (or before liquor).

Our tastes were certainly changing, though. At the end of World War II, American servicemen came home with a taste for Irish whiskey. There had really never been a market for it in the U.S. Most preferred American bourbon or Canadian whiskies—or even Scotch if they wanted something "foreign." But this became the period of the Irish.

A new drink that took America by storm was the Irish Coffee. It was first invented in Foynes, Ireland in the 1940s and brought to the U.S. in 1952. It became one of the most popular drinks of the decade and a staple in Irish bars and pubs all over the States.

About 20 years later, Bailey's Irish Cream was introduced into the U.S. market as well and became instantly popular. Bailey's is actually based on an old Irish tradition of drinking whiskey and cream to cure an upset stomach.

The crowning—though some would argue, distasteful—achievement came in 1979. That's when a bartender at a bar in Norwich, Connecticut invented the "Irish Car Bomb" drink: a shot of Bailey's Irish Cream and Jameson Irish Whiskey dropped into a pint of Guinness and then guzzled as fast as the person can drink. Trust us, don't order this one in Ireland ("car bomb" has a different meaning in Dublin).

Cocktails like the Irish Coffee, and even the Irish Car Bomb, represent true luxuries to Americans. Things were infinitely easier than they had been in the previous 50 years. There was no more war (not yet anyway), the economy was humming, and it was okay to drink. Americans began turning their attention to distractions, like sports.

In 1945, New England's Narragansett Beer was the first brewery to advertise on TV, sponsoring telecasts of Boston Red Sox games. It's kind of impossible to think of sporting events without sponsors (especially beer-related sponsors), but prior to this occasion, that's what it was like.

In fact, both parties were confused about how it actually should have worked. Should Narragansett pay according to the number of times they were mentioned or according to the sales as a result of the sponsorship?

In the end, believe it or not, it was just too hard to figure out, so the Red Sox didn't charge them at all. This was definitely a different time.

Television likewise was just beginning to grab a toehold in America (where the radio was still very popular). However, the televisions were expensive, and so not every family could afford them. Seizing on a great opportunity, bar-owners began buying and installing the televisions in their bars to attract customers who didn't have the novelty at home. In 1947 in Chicago, taverns and bars accounted for half of all television sales in the city.

Advertising in print was old hat by the 1960s, but sponsorships for television and radio were still relatively new, *and* cheap. In 1959, Strohs Beer pulled off a coup when it became the sole radio and television sponsor of the Detroit Tigers for a whopping $600,000. Even at the time that was a low price considering the amount of exposure they would get. But, as we said, the period was younger. They learned and it never happened again.

Sticking with the subject of advertising for a bit, in 1971 The New England Patriots were one of the first teams with a corporate sponsored stadium. The sponsor of course was Schaefer Brewing Co.

But the crowning achievement of booze-related sports marketing in the past fifty years, hell the past century, came care of the Cleveland Indians.

It was June 4th, 1974, and the Indians sucked. Their average game attendance the previous year was 8,000—understandable considering their record. On June 4th, though, they were hosting the Texas Rangers after losing to them amidst a fist-fight the week before.

Management came up with a brilliant incentive to get fans to the stadium. As much beer as you can drink for 10¢ per beer (in 8 ounce cups of course).

And it worked beautifully! The fans packed the stadium. And before long over 23,000 fans were guzzling to their hearts' content.

Meanwhile there was a game going on and Cleveland was again trailing. But the fans really didn't seem to notice. Not the woman who jumped onto the deck and flashed her boobs. Not the guy who streaked across the field. Not even the father and son team who jumped over the fence and mooned the crowd from infield.

But, then eventually the crowd turned its attention to the game again, specifically to the Texas players, who they pelted with hot dogs, cups, and whatever else they could find.

Then in the ninth inning, Cleveland looked to make a comeback. They'd made up a four point deficit and the scoring run was on base.

That's when a fan decided it'd be funny to run across the field and steal the hat off of outfielder Jeff Burroughs' head. In the process of confronting the idiot, Burroughs tripped.

The manager for the Rangers, seeing Burroughs fall down, sprang from the dugout thinking he'd been attacked and injured. In fact all of the Rangers sprung from the dugout (some with bats). Then the fans decided to take the field too. And many did. As a bonus, a lot of them had managed to pry up the metal seats they'd been sitting on and took those to the field also.

Needless to say, a riot ensued, with the Indians clearing the dugout to battle their own fans and protect the Texas players.

Finally, in the midst of the riot, chief ump Nestor Chylak called the game, and then got beaned in the head by a chair.

So, the moral of the story: cheap beer is good. Ten cent beer is great! Unlimited quantities of 10¢ beer might not be that good of an idea. It was a lesson Cleveland learned and limited all subsequent cheap beer nights to a 4-cup maximum.

Needless to say people loved their booze during this time. They loved buying it at bars and they loved drinking it. At some bars, though, not everyone was welcome.

McSorley's Old Ale House in New York City was the last of the "men only" pubs in the city, not allowing women until 1970 (though on a journey for our travel guides we discovered Palacio's Bar in Mesilla, New Mexico, which didn't allow women until 1990 and that was only after the original owner had passed away and his daughter took over).

Society's tastes were much like they were during any other period. *We simply enjoyed drinking.* This went for everybody from every walk of life. This was the time when celebrities like John Wayne would serve his favorite drink (Sauza Commemorativo Tequila) on his yacht over ice from an iceberg he once visited.

It was a time when professional wrestler Andre the Giant, at 7'4" and over 500 pounds, once drank 119 beers in 6 hours (which comes to one beer every three minutes nonstop).

It was a time when singer Tom Lehrer snuck vodka-spiked Jell-O onto an Air Force base in 1955, and later wrote about it, teaching college kids around the country how to make the "Jell-O shot."

Even Shirley Temple, the darling of the Silver Screen who'd had one of the most famous non-alcoholic drinks of all time named after her reportedly preferred vodka according to the National Enquirer.

It was a grand time to live, with a positive, forward-looking people and cheap booze. And then the politicians screwed virtually all of it up.

Things were going so well that in 1951 the ever helpful U.S. Congress raised the tax on a barrel of beer to $9 dollars. Bars had to raise the price of a glass 15¢ to make up for it.

This wasn't the last time in the past half-century they raised taxes on beer either. They actually ratcheted it up a little at a time over the years. Then, in 1991, the U.S. Federal Government doubled the taxes on a barrel of beer. Economists estimate this raise directly led to the loss of 60,000 jobs.

The government did do some things right, though (not much, but some). The term "Happy Hour" for example originated from the U.S. Navy, which would set aside an hour daily that was dedicated to rest and relaxation. It started being used by the public after a 1960 Saturday Evening Post article on the subject.

And while U.S. Senator, one of the booziest Presidents of the last 50 years, John F. Kennedy, invented and made fashionable the three-martini lunch. It would go *out* of style later when Jimmy Carter used it during a 1976 presidential debate as an example of how Americans were growing lazy compared to their foreign competitors. For his part President Ford retorted, saying that it showed the vigor of the American working man that he could down so much booze during lunch and then lead a productive workday afterwards.

In 1964 an act of Congress declared bourbon America's Native Spirit and the country's official spirit. Surprisingly Congress all got behind this one. It was not without controversy, however. While Native Americans were brewing a form of beer out of what came to be known as mash, later distilled into bourbon, many argue that rye was distilled earlier and should be recognized instead.

The year before Congress' rare show of solidarity where patriotism was concerned, Lyndon Johnson banned foreign wine from the White House and all U.S. embassies in 1963. Actually another good move, because American— specifically

"This here wine's made in 'merica!"

California—wines were beginning to become recognized for their quality. In fact the top selling sparkling wine in the U.S., Andre by Ernest and Juilo Gallo, was introduced only three years later in 1966 and was made in California.

And while Jimmy Carter did ruin lunch for just about all working Americans, he did redeem himself while President. In the U.S. home brewing was not permitted without paying excise tax until Jimmy Carter signed H.R. 1337 into law in October of 1978. The law permitted 100 gallons of beer per adult per year and up to a maximum of 200 gallons per household without paying excise taxes or posting a "penal bond."

It was a good thing this act was passed too, because this period was the period in which commercial beer production went to hell.

At this time many of the regional brewers in America were simply put out of business by the huge beer mega-brewers. Small, independent but quality breweries like People's Beer in Oshkosh, Wisconsin, the first brewery to be owned by an African American from 1970-1972, simply couldn't match the goliath brewers' marketing or distribution.

A quick study of the growth of one of these brewers will demonstrate what the small ones were up against. Under the direction of Fred Miller, Miller Brewing Company, for example, went from producing 800,000 barrels a year in 1953, to 3 million in 1958.

That was nothing compared to its success in the 1970s. Miller Lite's, "Taste Great Less Filling" campaign drove sales from 7 million barrels per year to 31 million barrels per year from 1973-1978.

Of course by this time the Millers had nothing to do with Miller Brewing. In 1966 Lorraine John Mulberger (heiress of the Miller brewing fortune) sold the majority of her family's business because she objected to alcohol. We're sure the thirty million she got from the devil drink was enough to clear her conscious though.

Brewing in this period became less about good beer and more about marketing and gimmicks. Innovation no longer meant better tasting products, simply lower costs. Like Coors for example, which at one time provided new and exciting beer to its customers. One of its major contributions to the industry during this time was the two-piece, seamless aluminum beer can to replace the more expensive steel can. Wow.

From a cost-perspective this made sense. After all, from 1935-1980, packaged beer sales grew from 30% to 88% of industry sales (tap beer meanwhile shrank from 70% to 12%).

Beer sales in general, though, were declining. Even with the population growth after World War II, per capita beer consumption did not reach pre-Prohibition levels until 1970.

What was the cause of such a decline? Obviously it wasn't output—the brewers were putting out plenty of product. It couldn't have been the economy. After all, Americans never had it as well as they did in the 1950s and 1960s.

Maybe it was the type, variety and quality of beer that led to the slow growth in the industry.

Think about this. In 1983 there were only 80 breweries left in the United States. The largest six accounted for 92% of the beer production in the country.

It's no wonder that people like Jack McAuliffe of Sonoma, California decided to do something different. In 1976 Jack opened the New Albion Brewing Company, reportedly the first micro-brewery of the Modern Era. Craft and micro-brewery has made a comeback around the world, and quality beer is once again available in just about every grocer across the U.S.

Before we leave this period, and our history, we need to reflect a moment on the feats that occurred in drinking beer. In the last half century, the world record for drinking beer the fastest had been set and then shattered time and again.

In 1955 it was by an Australian university student who was forced to down 2.5 pints of beer as punishment for violating one of his school's rules. The young student, Bob Hawke, set a record by drinking the 2.5 pints of beer in 11 seconds. God Bless the Aussies, they elected him Prime Minister in 1983.

The real record, though, was set in 1977. That's when Steven Petrosino, a graduate student and soon to be Marine Corps Officer, set the world speed record for beer drinking when he drank one liter of beer in 1.3 seconds.

There's so much more to write about, so much more to say about our past, our drunken history, and our culture's love—maybe our species' love—for alcohol. It's been a part of our lives for 10,000 plus years. It's affected how we've lived, where we've lived, and why we've lived.

Anything written will fall short somewhere. A book will focus on this but not on that. It will look at the statistics of America, but no France. This is inevitable considering the subject is so closely related to our evolution.

We've tried, though, to give a brief history of us (meaning man/human-kind) at it relates to booze. And what have we perhaps learned? Only this: it's a part of us. It's our humanity.

Afterword

The concept of Drunken History was started years ago when the authors, who love to travel, were gearing up for a trip to the Big Apple. Excited to be going to one of America's oldest cities they scoured travel guides and the internet looking for historical bars to visit. What they found was a lack of information not only on historical bars in and around New York but also on mankind's historical involvement with fermentation and distillation.

A couple of years after their trip to New York the authors decided it would be a great idea to research, travel to and share the facts of both alcohol's history and some of the great historic bars still present today. So Drunken History was born as a medium for sharing and celebrating man's historical quest for, development of, and infatuation with liquid libations with the world.

Drunken History, the Book, is the first in a series of books and Travel Guides about alcohol and history. Quickly following its release the authors will be releasing the must read book, "Bucket List Bars."

Bucket List Bars is the first in a multi-part travel guide series about historic bars still open today. It tells the history of each establishment, what it was like in the past, what it is like today, what it means and meant to its patrons, must-try drinks and food, great events, and when and how to get there. It is a new and modern guide and includes QR codes that when scanned will show videos about the bar and how to get there.

Writing this book was an adventure the authors will not soon forget. Thank you for joining us on this journey through the world's historic adventures with fermented and distilled spirits. And remember the next time that you pick up that pint of beer, shot of whiskey, or glass of Scotch, you're about to drink history. Cheers!

Connect with us!

Online:	http://www.drunkenhistory.com
On Twitter:	@DrunkenHistory
On Facebook:	Facebook.com/drunkenhistory
On Foursquare:	Foursquare.com/drunkenhistory
On Pinterest:	Pinterest.com/drunkenhistory

Don't miss out on our upcoming guide,

Bucket List Bars,

The Historic Saloons, Taverns, Pubs and Dives of America

Made in the USA
Lexington, KY
05 June 2014